T0322336

LET HEALING HAPPEN

LET HEALING HAPPEN

A SHAMANIC GUIDE TO LIVING AN AUTHENTIC AND HAPPY LIFE

EDDY ELSEY

RIDER

1

Rider, an imprint of Ebury Publishing
20 Vauxhall Bridge Road
London SW1V 2SA

Rider is part of the Penguin Random House group of companies
whose addresses can be found at global.penguinrandomhouse.com

First published by Rider in 2024

www.penguin.co.uk

A CIP catalogue record for this book is available from the British Library

ISBN 9781846047534

Typeset in 12.5/17.5pt Adobe Garamond Pro by Jouve (UK), Milton Keynes
Printed and bound in Great Britain by Clays Ltd, Elcograf S.p.A.

The authorised representative in the EEA is Penguin Random House Ireland,
Morrison Chambers, 32 Nassau Street, Dublin D02 YH68

Penguin Random House is committed to a sustainable future
for our business, our readers and our planet. This book is made
from Forest Stewardship Council® certified paper.

A prayer of gratitude to earth-centric cultures worldwide who have fought to keep their traditions alive and graciously shared them with the West.

Inspired by these incredible teachings, my prayer is that we are able to plant the seeds of our own earth-centric traditions so that we can become stewards of the natural world, and remember how to restore our own innate harmony.

CONTENTS

INTRODUCTION

Growing up in North London in the 1990s and early 2000s, I dreamt of becoming many things, but I can honestly say that a shamanic healer was not one of them. But life has a funny way of taking us on twists and turns and, despite my unspiritual and agnostic beginnings, I stumbled across the mysterious and wonderful world of shamanic practice in my early twenties. Almost a decade later, my entire life has been dedicated to shamanism and other earth-centric forms of spirituality. If I was to name my overriding passion in life, it is to find ways to bridge the gap between authentic, and often ancient, forms of earth worship and our disconnected modern lives. Despite how alien this felt to me as a young man, to my surroundings and my upbringing, I was astonished at how effective it was in enabling me to put myself back together psychologically after suffering my entire life from acute anxiety and OCD.

As a practice and belief system, shamanism provides the framework in which we can connect ourselves with the earth. This, as we shall see, is a crucial element of healing in the West. In shamanic belief, a key reason that the modern world suffers from so many mental and physical health conditions is due to the great separation between us and the natural world. Our modern culture has become so severed from a natural way of living that we are now starting to experience a huge amount of imbalances in our physiological and psychological states. Increasingly, we are finding that we are unable to feel rested, joyful and at peace. From these states of imbalance, each of us learn to build a life as best we can around our personal suffering and call it 'fate', without ever understanding what it feels like to be held and safe and to explore the full range of our humanity.

I have worked with over a thousand individuals one-to-one, in groups, in retreats and in workshops, and I am yet to see a person who doesn't benefit in a great way from learning the shamanic principles in this book and applying them to their everyday modern life. One of the great gifts of shamanic practice is that the framework it gives can be applied to any of us, whether we class ourselves as spiritual or not. This is a grounded and experiential form of spirituality that has survived from the wild and ruthless Stone Age, to the boundary-pushing, fast-paced modern day, and it is just as effective a practice today as it was in the distant past, due to its incredibly adaptable and malleable characteristics. Shamanism is remarkably human – so much so that shamanic practitioners and shamanic cultures have erupted from the earth in many of the habitable continents – despite not having contact with one another.

This is the first teaching of this book – that although our cultures wax and wane like the moon in the sky, the land beneath our feet still pulses with the same power that it always has. Shamanism is a gateway into the mysterious world of that power.

This book will not teach you to become a shaman. Instead, it seeks to give you an overview of shamanic and animistic practice (see page 11 for how I define these practices). It will share some of the foundational beliefs that unite shamanic practices worldwide so that you will be able to live your life from a more shamanic viewpoint, and enable you to become an animist, or shamanist, yourself – a person who follows an animist or shamanic way of life and believes in the worldview of earth-centric cultures who still practise animism and shamanism. All people who have faith in, and a small knowledge of, the animist and shamanic concepts in this book are capable of small feats of folk magic, personal protective and healing rituals, and of learning how to stay in balance with the natural world. The rituals at the end of each chapter are inspired by these collective forms of ceremony and, although powerful, are safe and can be done by anybody without initiation. The overall purpose of this book is to 'shamanically inspire' you, so that you feel that no matter where you are from, or what you do, that this is a practice that is available to you.

I hope that you will start to feel it is not only possible to heal your pain and find balance, but that you can also understand you are an important part of this beautiful world.

This book is part memoir, part self-help guide, part anthropological account and part mission. The difference between this book and other spiritual books is that, although many of the teachings in this book seem estranged from the modern world, I am steadfast in my encouragement for you to remain as much a part of modern Western culture as possible. I am of the firm belief that it is by breathing life into our already existing culture that we will be able to start to rebalance and heal ourselves. If we learn to balance the undoubted ecstasy and magic of the spiritual path with the rational, mundane experience of the everyday then we can learn to approach life from a grounded perspective. It is this crystal clarity and deep, human wisdom that shamanism can provide.

Some of the cultures mentioned in this book I have spent personal time with – the Wixárika of Mexico, the Black Darkhad of Mongolia, the Iwol of Senegal – and some I have studied from afar. The main aim of cross-referencing our modern culture with the traditions of these indigenous cultures is not just to illustrate their effective and ingenious forms of ritual, healing and initiation, but also to find the common human threads that exist in both their cultures and ours. It is then by discovering these threads that connect our modern lives to traditional cultures that we can use them as guidelines to make these incredibly effective healing practices relevant to our contemporary existence.

Alongside this, we will also explore the Western New Age spiritual culture and where our current spiritual culture differs greatly from more traditional ones. Genuine practices of spirituality have been refined over hundreds or thousands of years – often with great sacrifices incurred to ensure that a spiritual culture moves forward in the correct way. The New Age does not have this luxury, and we are very early on in our spiritual explorations in the West. Due to this there are many blind spots and dead-ends that exist within Western New Age culture. My personal spiritual journey began in the New Age culture in the West and this didn't work out very well for me (we will take a look at this tumultuous journey later on). I ended up turning to, and taking refuge in, the safety of the lineages of tried and tested spiritual traditions. The mishmash of practices that make up the New Age – light language, crystal healing, diluted yoga and meditation – and some much newer and looser forms of Western shamanism – untested energy healing techniques and irresponsibly held plant medicine ceremonies – all combined with the lack of regulation and shortage of verified elders to guide these experiences, create a maelstrom of spiritual experience where many end up worse off than they were when they began. In my experience, many people are getting burnt by this, and I will seek in this book to constructively point out some ways that we could navigate ourselves out of the New Age and practise more effective and safer ways of spirituality. While at some point we will likely develop our own authentic spiritual culture in the West, we are incredibly fortunate to still have access to authentic traditions, and I will outline a comparison to these traditions and to the New Age to illustrate my criticisms.

On a more positive note, the undeniably exciting element of the New Age exploding in popularity in the West, especially over the last few decades, is that it proves the huge hunger we have for spiritual nourishment. Our souls are eager for connection on a deeper level and many are drawn to the alluring power of spirituality to provide this. But this is not limited to those who fit in with the typical spiritual paradigm. Even those who consider themselves 'unspiritual' are magnetised towards tribe and community through subcultures that help satiate the inherent human need for belonging and expression. Before my spiritual journey it was dance music and football, but for others it may be online gaming, yoga, tattooing, pop culture or heavy metal. These subcultures hold a lot of power for us in the West, and when people get together with a shared intention, this power is amplified. Where there is power, there is the potential for transformation and healing, but, on the other side of the coin, also destruction and trauma. Without a communal spiritual practice like shamanism present in our culture we have forgotten how to work with big collective energies and this is part of the reason why we often see the darker sides of our subcultures periodically unleashed – seemingly without warning. Some form of violence and abuse is present in all Western subcultures, and I believe that shamanism, as a community-based practice, can provide us with the tools of how to work with large amounts of communal energy and help us to remain balanced within its power. Modern Western culture is vibrant, emergent and exciting, and I believe that we can start to work with this power to begin to spiritually re-empower our culture if we can learn the spiritual mechanics that underly communal human behaviour.

For all the magic and wonder of the spiritual path, the single most important lesson I have learnt about spirituality is that it has to be down-to-earth. We must be able to integrate our spiritual practices, and wisdom gleaned from them, into our everyday life. It's easy to be spiritual on a retreat, but much more difficult when you're stressed out amidst the chaos of life. Similarly, if our spiritual path takes us away from our everyday duties, and makes it more difficult for us to deal with our everyday problems, we need to rethink if it is truly something that is beneficial to us. I danced with this dichotomy during my own journey, and in the desire to become as spiritual as possible, as fast as possible, I decided to leave behind a lot of the things that kept me in touch with reality. I went from a North

London 'lad' to a holier-than-thou spiritual practitioner without doing the necessary work to integrate the former with the latter, and while there is humour in remembering this period in my life, my lack of authenticity led me into an intense mental breakdown that my spiritual practices at the time made much worse. I descended into extraordinary levels of excessive magical thinking and huge levels of paranoia that masqueraded as spiritual enlightenment. The further that I went down the rabbit hole, the more isolated I became and the more spiritual I believed I was becoming. This cycle reached breaking point as I was completely consumed with intrusive thoughts and ended up contemplating suicide to liberate myself from my own darkness. I dedicate a whole chapter to explain this process and how we can avoid it by keeping our feet on the ground. The mundane world is very much your ally and friend on your spiritual journey, which is unfortunately a sentiment that is often missed in Western spiritual communities.

Many stories will be told in this book, both personal and collective. Our entire lives are woven together by stories. The story of who we are, of who others are in relation to us, and the story of our relationship with the wider world. Often forgotten in our modern world is how large a part our ancestral story plays in our lives too. That our precious lives add new pages into the story book of our bloodline, begun by members of our families who came long before us, and continued by those who will exist long after us – all who each have their own stories too. All of this beautiful complexity must be taken into account when looking at healing, and we will explore the elegant concepts that shamanism offers and the important factor that mythology and symbolism play when working with ourselves internally. It is important to note here that shamanism is *much* more than just a psychological or symbolic exercise. Indigenous cultures understand that the earth can speak to us *directly* through symbolism and myth, and a big part of coming back into relationship with the earth again is learning the way to allow her song to charm our ears and to recognise when she is speaking to us. This is a very important skill that we have forgotten in the West, and the issues related to a cultural disconnection from this earth-speech cannot be underestimated. The shamanic concept of offerings, as well as the art of prayer, is key here. These are both the currency and the main communication method for humans to contact, honour and begin to work with the earth. We must learn to do this so that we can start to repair the debt caused by our modern lives that, up to this date, have consumed far more than we have given back.

But . . .

How do all these concepts work in our modern world, and what good does it do to look backwards to older times, or to cultures that some may deem as 'less advanced than ours'?

Firstly, we must understand that there are two types of

technology. Scientific and spiritual. The West, although well versed in science, is lacking in spiritual technology. In order to prevent our scientific technology from consuming us, we must develop our spiritual consciousness to meet it. This is a process of learning to take into account the wisdom of our hearts alongside our minds. In the face of great upheaval and transition on earth, our science will not save us unless we begin to work on our spirit.

Finally, while I have practised and trained in yoga, tantra and meditation too, this book will focus on shamanism and other earth-centric forms of spirituality. From a Western perspective I believe this makes the most sense, because – from the very beginning of humanity up until only 800 years ago – most of us would have been pagan, animistic or shamanistic in our beliefs. I believe there are several reasons that these earth-centric forms of worship are making their way back into mainstream consciousness, as I will explain in the following chapter.

This book is for everyone. Another great benefit of shamanic practices is the freedom of expression that they bring and the great joy and beauty of being part of life that they encourage. They are expansive forms of worship, rather than restrictive. I believe that this encourages us to start to come to terms with the fact that the human experience, no matter who we are, is inherently a spiritual one. After all, are we not all searching for community, connection and purpose? I suppose that makes us all a big, spiritual, human family.

This book has been inspired by my own journey through life up to this point, my explorations into spirituality, and my learnings and teachings so far. I am no different to you. I am not so much wiser for the last decade of spiritual practice, or special for it. I have made many mistakes, and despite my best intentions I am sure I will continue to do so. Many, if not all, of the ideas within this book are inspired by others, and even those thoughts that seemed to drop into my mind out of the blue have, I'm sure, rattled around the heads of many others over time.

Although I will talk about spirits, energy and the like in this book, you do not have to believe in these things to read it. I do not seek to push any ideas and beliefs onto you, or ridicule you for ideas and beliefs you already have. This book is about personal and community spiritual healing, and coming back into a harmonious relationship with ourselves and the land so that we can find the beauty in this world again.

The messages in this book are simple, but effective, and I hope, whoever you are, that you feel seen when you read my words.

SHAMANISM AND ANIMISM

In the West, there seems to be a lot of confusion about what shamanism is.

It is a term that seems to flit and jump around with a life of its own, which, as we will discover, is probably quite appropriate.

To understand shamanism, we must first understand the worldview and practice that shamanism evolved from – animism. All corners of the globe, from South America to Northern Asia, Europe to India, Australasia to North America and beyond have animist roots. Animism is the first form of spirituality that ever existed, and it revolves around the core belief that everything in existence is alive. Nothing is considered dead within the animist worldview, and animals, places, objects, sicknesses, words, even ideas, beliefs and human-created objects such as machines and houses are seen to have their own souls. Cultures such as the North American traditions, the Aboriginal Australians, the many South American traditions and the ancient Celts, Norse and Saxons of Europe are examples of animist cultures.

Animist cultures are typically very ceremonial and have many rituals that create sacred containers in which quite miraculous healing can happen. In animist cultures, the healer's main role is to understand how to create these containers, and they do this through prayer and invocations, dancing, chanting or something else focussed and repetitive. Animism, in my opinion, is the most human of all spiritual practices. This is proven by the fact that all pockets of humans, no matter where in the world they existed, developed remarkably similar forms of animist beliefs and techniques. Animism can be seen as the first spark of all spiritual concept, all community ritual and all transpersonal healing.

In some parts of the world, mostly around Central and Northern Asia, shamanism developed out of animism (this was the case in Siberia, Tibet and Mongolia, for example). The main difference between animism and shamanism is that while animist cultures have incredibly powerful ceremonial healers, a shamanic culture has dedicated healers – the shamans – who have developed the capacity to invoke spirit possession at will, and undertake 'spiritual flights'. It is by invoking these possession states that they are able to commune with spirits and travel to 'other-worlds' where they are able to manipulate non-ordinary reality in order to create change in our ordinary reality.

Some anthropologists also describe the plant medicine cultures of the Amazon and Central America as shamanic, as they too work within deep altered states of conscious-ness by ingesting their sacred psychoactive plants. I tend to agree with this statement, but some others do not. There have also been shamanic cultures found in small pockets of West Africa, Hungary, north-western America, Finland, Norway and Russia.

While all animist cultures employ altered states of con-sciousness in some way, it is the use and masterful control of the trance and possession state that sets shamanic cultures apart from their animist counterparts. A skilled shaman can invoke their ancestors and certain powerful nature spirits in order to assist their communities in incredible ways. While animism and shamanism both include some astrological wisdom in their practices, in my experience shamanic cultures have developed more intricate systems of astrological calculation that are based on highly complex mathematical equations. This enables them, in my opinion, to work with more accuracy. To become a shaman one must be born a shaman, and become verified by another shaman. A person will often undergo a 'shamanic sickness' before they are initiated – as they are unable to control the fierce shamanic spirits that they are connected to. It is a difficult role and a huge responsibility.

Earth-Centric Worship

While there are differences between animism and shamanism, within the shamanic community a little too much effort goes into highlighting them, in my opinion, and it is important that we do not get too bogged down in definitions in this moment of spiritual exploration in the West. While I am fully in support of protecting the authenticity of each practice, and to take care in not mindlessly blending them together, in the West we are in a peculiar position of finding ways to birth an authentic culture to our lands after we lost our own animist and shamanic practices to the mists of time.

For this reason, I think it is important to view all of these forms of worship as equally valuable and powerful. After all, the exclusion of what is animist and what is shamanic is not, and never has been, black and white. All the cultures deemed to be animist have elements of shamanism running through them – trance, healing and nature worship, and all shamanic cultures are based upon animist worldviews. It is now our job in the West to learn as much as we can about both of these practices so that we can sow authentic seeds in our own lands for our own earth-centric culture to flourish.

Why now? The Spiritualities of Survival

One of the great virtues of animist and shamanic practice is that they are malleable practices that assist humans wherever they choose to settle. While our lives are different in virtually every way to our hunter-gatherer and agrarian ancestors, we can still access the same healing benefits that these practices provided them. This is because both shamanism and animism are spiritual practices that are concerned with survival, which is why they are the only forms of worship that have survived from the beginning of humanity up to the modern day.

They are adaptive, resilient and, at their core, based around human community and relationship.

The Stone Age hunter-gatherers who first developed

these practices were not focussed on enlightenment, but on making their worldly lives easier. The aims of both animism and shamanism are simply to restore balance in life where it has become imbalanced. By doing this they enable people to live harmoniously with one another and the natural landscape around them.

Although our problems may have changed, the benefits of the practices themselves have not. They offer us real solutions to the real-world problems of our day. It is no coincidence, I feel, that a spiritual practice concerned with survival has begun to erupt in the collective consciousnesses of the modern West, at the same time that we must navigate one of our most perilous time of existence. As global warming looms ever closer, it is shamanism and animism that may provide us with solutions, and in Chapter 9 I will outline my argument as to why I believe so.

THE MODERN REVIVAL OF SHAMANISM

I was not surprised to read a recent *Guardian* article (by Robert Booth, Carmen Aguilar García and Pamela Duncan) explaining that shamanism is Britain's fastest-growing religion. This practice offers a very empowering stance on spirituality and healing. It doesn't just facilitate recovery from our symptoms of mental and physical unease, but it offers us the opportunity to take back the personal power that has been lost through experiencing trauma and sickness. As a community-based practice, it is collaborative at its core, and although the shaman may lead the way, you will also undertake a journey yourself. While allopathic medicine can be miraculous, and capable of incredible feats of healing, it can often lack an empowering aspect. We are used to handing ourselves over to doctors and surgeons and letting them get to work. This can have wonderful benefits, but a big part of long-term healing is the experiential understanding of our own personal power and the unique human life force that runs through each one of us – which is something that modern medicine often does not facilitate. Similarly, other spiritual paths – particularly certain forms of modern-day and New Age spirituality – offer us words and guidance but no lived experience. This makes them hard to anchor too, as they become too mind-based and not somatic enough. Earth-centric spirituality is about direct experience as well as intellectual theory. This, I think, makes it a unique form of healing.

Another reason people are becoming drawn to shamanism is that, as a practice, it taps into beliefs and sensations that already reside inside of us. Shamanism works with the natural elements and the spirits that empower them. While believing in spirits may be a stretch for some people, all of us can acknowledge how our mood lifts when we feel the sun on our face, or how our ears prick up at the sound of a howling gale. The pitter-patter of rain may bring us joy or despair but it makes us feel *something*, and everyone, from my hippy friends to my dad's mates, understands the soothing benefits of a nice long walk in nature, away from the hustle of the city. These are the gateways to the spirituality that shamanism offers, and – whether you choose to believe in the spirits that inhabit them or not – you can utilise shamanic practice to enhance your relationship with these forces to find balance and calm amidst chaos.

We will explore all of this and more within this book. But first, let's address healing from an earth-centric perspective.

CHAPTER 1

Embarking on Your Journey
to Healing

Before reading this chapter I encourage you, wherever you are, to take a moment for yourself. A quiet, considered and conscious moment, just for you.
Gently coming to a comfortable position and resting your eyelids together, take a deep breath down into the centre of your being and settle into yourself.

The very fact that you have picked up this book and got this far means that, in some way, there is a yearning to heal. Perhaps this is a large yearning and you have been on this journey for quite some time, or perhaps there is a small muttering that bubbles up from your soul that is trying to tell you that things aren't quite as good as they could be. Either way this can be an uncomfortable, excitable, mysterious feeling – like simultaneously pining for a great adventure yet wondering if you may get flattened as soon as you leave your front door. I believe that an innate desire to find the spark that will reawaken us towards a more meaningful existence exists within all of us. It's a human thing.

But although this book is about healing, life is not. Life is about existing naturally in the organic and balanced way that nature functions. Healing, then, in the way that is meant in this book, is about dusting off the old pathways that lead us back to that balance. It is important we remember that healing is not the *goal* in life, but the necessary step that we must sometimes take when we find ourselves stranded away from where we feel we are meant to be. Like all good journeys, the route is arduous, but, if we remember to look up every now and then, it can also be full of wonder. Healing takes surrender and vulnerability, but also action, and will, and learning when to push and when to let go and move on are all essential parts of the process.

In my shamanic healing practice, people often come to me from a place of exasperation. They have smoked their habits right to the filter, wrung out their coping mechanisms until the rag is dry, and are just about keeping themselves from collapsing in a heap, teetering on the edge of giving up completely and allowing themselves to be consumed by the world. In less poetic terms they are riddled with anxiety, numb with depression, or utterly consumed with obsessive tendencies. Their bodies may be chronically sick, and there is often a vacantness within their minds that points towards a severe level of disconnection from the world around them.

I can recognise it in others because I have felt the same. I spent much of my life feeling completely lost, with no real sense of vitality or inner joyfulness. I was close to breaking point, and it felt almost impossible to muster the strength that was needed to get stuck in amongst this wonderful world and make my mark. When we feel this way, it is as if we have become zombified, desperately searching for something that will break us through the haze of torpidity that follows us around like a cold chill.

It's not a very nice place to be, and there are many, many ways that we can end up here. To talk about healing means to first talk about sickness, and, in shamanic belief, sickness can occur for many reasons.

The difference between shamanic belief and the typical Western view of sickness is that – while both agree on the idea that for us to fall sick means to fall prey to a sickness itself – shamanic belief states that for the 'physical' symptom of sickness to arrive, there is a pre-existing internal or spiritual imbalance, which has created the conditions for this external sickness to take root. In shamanism, sickness does not arrive spontaneously, but begins to fester due to an imbalance in our internal environment. This internal imbalance causes a loss of our own innate spiritual and energetic power, which acts much like our immune system – fending off disease before it grows large enough to take us over.

As the healer, it is the shaman's job to diagnose the

original cause of the imbalance and then re-establish balance by removing or mitigating the effects of it, often through ceremony and working directly with their helper spirits, but sometimes through herbs or encouraging a shift in behaviour for the person who is suffering. The original causes could be anything from a traumatic experience, a dysfunctional childhood, a disturbance in nature or becoming a victim of a curse or spiritual entity, inheriting ancestral trauma, a lack of proper diet or improper behaviour. In shamanic belief, even too much technological stimulus can cause imbalances that eventually lead to sickness. Once this root cause has been addressed, a shaman will then return a person's spiritual and energetic power. Over time, and depending on the severity of the issues faced, this restores the harmony within a person's physical, energetic and spiritual systems. It is then down to the person to live in a way that tends to this harmony like a garden. In this way, a healthy person is an ecosystem.

That being said, as imperfect humans in an imperfect world, it is not realistic to live our entire lives in perfect balance and harmony. Sicknesses, and the imbalances that create them, are impossible to escape, and all of us will suffer at some point, in some way, during our existence.

What we can do, however, is do our best to stay as close to balance as possible, so that healing remains an option for us. This book is about how to do that.

THE WESTERN IMBALANCE

We live in a time, in the West, where we are more discon-nected from the earth than ever before. Due to this disconnection, an unhealthy sense of individuality and chronic loneliness has spread through our culture like wildfire. This inevitably leads to behaviours that create fur-ther imbalances and compound sickness. An example of this would be a person turning to drink and drugs as a way to numb the pain of a tumultuous childhood. Whereas a Western form of healing may look like sending the person to rehab, a shamanic outlook would focus on address-ing the imbalances caused by the childhood, or even to look to the ancestral reasons to why the parents acted the way that they did. While rehab is effective and may work short-term, without diagnosing and healing the original imbalance that led to the destructive behaviour and addict-ive tendencies, there is a high chance that a person will be driven again by the root issue to relapse. Just like a weed in the garden, without removing the root ball it will continue to grow. Studies reflect this, and 85 per cent of individuals relapse within one year of rehabilitation. But by diagnos-ing and healing the root cause of addiction (trauma and loneliness), instead of focussing as much on the final symptom of the imbalance (addiction and substances), a shaman is able to heal the original damage and free an addict from the primal wound that caused a need for addictive tendencies.

Although this is just one example, the majority of the sicknesses that we face in the West can ultimately be traced back to intense feelings of tension in the body and isolation in the mind. In shamanic healing, our destructive behaviours, anxieties, depressions and obsessive disorders are seen as attempts to numb the pain of these feelings, and our chronic and acute sicknesses are the results of them.

But although many people suffer trauma and pain, why is it that the rates of chronic and acute mental and physical illnesses are higher in Westernised countries than anywhere else globally?

The answer, shamanic teachings say, is not that we are in some way intrinsically different, but simply that we do not have a strong enough relationship with the land and the forces that inhabit it. We are detached, adrift and therefore alone – cut off from the natural umbilical cord of earthly nourishment and connection. While this has caused imbalances, what is even more a tragedy is that we have lost our ability to heal them. Over time, our cultural disconnection has led to the tragic loss of the wisdom of earth-centric worship, and – without this wisdom, and the knowledge of correct ritual, healing and behaviour that it includes – we have no ceremonial remedies to transmute the traumas we each face back into the earth and renew ourselves. With no understanding of how to rebalance ourselves, no deeper perspectives around sickness and healing, and no way to heal the spiritual and energetic issues we face – they stay locked inside our bodies and minds like intense electrical charges, creating huge amounts of tension until something inevitably snaps and a myriad of uncomfortable symptoms arise.

THE THREE STAGES OF HEALING

As imbalances inevitably find us, we will all go through periods of our life when we are called to renew ourselves. We may not heed that call, and instead seek to distract ourselves and turn the other way – but, if we choose to, and have enough commitment, we can undertake a journey to reclaim the parts of us that have gone awry and restore a sense of balance in ourselves. This journey can often seem incredibly disorganised and chaotic – but this doesn't need to be the case. We are fortunate that this process has been mapped cross-culturally by traditional cultures, and by the ethnographers and anthropologists who studied them – like the great Arnold van Gennep and Victor Turner. As we shall explore, traditional cultures from around the world – the Iwol in Senegal, the Sateré-Mawé in Brazil, the Powhatan people of the Algonquin nation, to name a few – understand the essential nature of personal growth and of transitioning into new ways of being, and encourage this process in their cultures from a young age. In fact, they see it as so important that, instead of waiting for the moment when healing becomes an absolute necessity (as we often do in the West), members of their culture are forced into difficult and intricate rites of passage at adolescence, making sure that their youth heal any childhood issues before crossing over into adulthood. In fact, it is often the case that they will not be considered as real adults unless they complete the rites of passage and successfully emerge on the other side. While our day-to-day lives are very different to those of our indigenous cousins, the actual process of healing – the underlying mechanisms of the psyche during the healing journey – is the same for all humans.

In the West we are now starting to understand that all transitional periods in our life can bring great difficulties and obstacles for us. Birth, teenagehood, adulthood, middle age and death are all unavoidable transitions, and many others experience crisis after marriage and childbirth. Each of us may also face our own traumas that erupt at certain moments in our life and call us to the gates of growth and change. It is a great misfortune that in the West we have lost our traditional rites of passage that assist us in safely navigating these transitional periods, but we can still facilitate the process for ourselves by learning the necessary concepts and creating space for healing to occur. It is of vital importance that we do this, as the health of a culture depends on its ability to mark and navigate transition so that those within it can access deeper clarity, wisdom and renewal rather than descending into disorientation, becoming prisoners of their own delusion, greed and anger.

Therefore, by learning these three distinct stages to the transitional process we can start to make sense of these tricky moments in our lives. These stages are severance, liminality and aggregation. They involve a loss of self, the stepping into the unknown, and then a triumphant return to life, having been renewed in some way and rendered more complete, with a 'fuller' sense of identity.

Although the symptoms of transition can manifest in many different ways – some small and less daunting, and some so huge that they feel as though they will swallow us whole – if we can begin to understand that transition is not just a difficult situation but a completely necessary factor in growth, this can give us the confidence that we will emerge from our healing crisis and not become consumed by it.

Stage One of Healing: Severance

Severance, the first stage, brings a loss of identity. This is essential, as to be reborn we first need to die. This death, although psychospiritual and not literal, can feel very, very real. Often the survival mechanisms within each of our personalities can't tell the difference between the literal and the symbolic, and the emotions that can arise at this stage are strong and urgent. In the West we are often not taught that much of our psychological structure is symbolic, and much vaster than the personality that we identify with. We tend to identify completely with our immediate feelings, instead of understanding that we are much more than our different sub-personality structures – the characters inside of us – which each have different behaviours, needs and wants. Due to this, when a healing crisis emerges we become completely identified with the urgency of the survival sub-personalities that arise in response to it, and are unable to recognise the soul's calling that is pushing for acknowledgement and seeking to emerge underneath them. Instead, we focus mainly on the fear and inadequacy of the limited, but loud, aspects of our personalities that spring forth in the face of great change. Therefore, during a time of severance it is common for it to *seem* as though if we don't further tense up and protect ourselves and our identity, we might even cease to exist altogether. This brings with it a huge amount of fear of something worse than death itself – complete annihilation and non-being. If we identify too much with this, our mental health symptoms may feel as though they are getting worse, and our various neuroses get louder and more intense as the parts of our personalities that we are shedding hold on for dear life. Within the animist worldview, these parts of our personalities are alive, and, like anything else that lives, they want to stay alive. An internal tug-of-war ensues, but however painful this experience, we must remember that this can be a logical response to inner change. Our sense of safety in the world is based around our personal identity, and our personal boundaries are built around what we believe we are and what we believe we are capable of. When something begins to encroach upon these boundaries, and when what we believe we are starts to feel fragile and false, it is terrifying and disorientating. All signals point towards doubling down and holding on to whatever identity we have left in these moments. This could manifest in huge amounts of paranoia and feeling as though our life as we know it is over. There is a tendency here to isolate ourselves out of shame and the fear that other people will think we are crazy. But what we must do is the opposite. Symbolically this is the point in which we must leave the nest. Perhaps you can imagine the great fear of a newborn chick who is about to embark on their first flight. Peering over the edge of the nest – all that it has ever known – and looking outward into the chasms of the wider world, where many dangers await them. But they have wings for a reason. If they are to fulfil their destiny, they must risk flight, which also means – in some way – to risk death.

There is a propensity to hark back to the past at this stage of our journey. Even though we may know on a deeper level that there is a sacred signal for change that we cannot ignore, we desire to go backwards and return to the childlike naivety that cocooned us in the false security of the past. Even if we know that the past was accompanied by distress and pain, it is somehow more familiar and comforting than the great unknown and potential annihi-lation. We may feel that to accept the call and move into the next stage would overwhelm and consume us completely. But we must be aware that it is not the pain that is getting worse, but that the illusion of safety is diminishing. The amount of pain is the same, but the illusions we used to dis-tract ourselves from it are starting to fail. This is a *very* good thing. Nothing good comes from living in illusion, and, although confronting our pain seems like the last thing that we want to do, we will be rewarded by moving forward.

The aim of initiatory rites in traditional cultures is twofold. One aim is to forge a child into an adult, and the other is to induct a person into a certain role in the community. These things often go hand-in-hand, as a member of that tribe will be asked to prove themselves before they are given responsi-bility for others. When we have responsibility, we have power, and the rites of passage are set up to make sure that the initiates go through a deep process of change, that any childlike personas and habits that could cause harm to themselves and others, once they have access to this power, are left in the past. These include (as we have spoken about already) any false identities and delusion. To be forged in the fires of initiation and confront the pain and traumas of the past allows a person to connect to their deeper self and learn to wield responsibility with compassion and care. A person who conquers their demons has much less chance of becoming one. It is a great shame that these rites of passage have been lost in the modern West, for as we grow, no matter where our lives take us, we all begin to gain access to more responsibility and power. A child acting out may be seen as annoying, but an adult who does the same is potentially dangerous – both to themselves and to others. The process of initiation and healing is also the process of learning how to live in right relation with the world around us – with compassion, maturity and care.

Traditional initiation rituals involve methods that would make you wince. In certain communities of aboriginal Australia they included ritual circumcision and scarification of their young men and women. Wounds were ritually opened on their chest, buttocks, shoulders, arms and – for men – the underside of their penis. Sometimes these wounds were filled with magical items. This was said to give the youth enough strength to move into adulthood. These scars represented the ordeal undertaken and also gave them a sense of power, as they are said to have been imbued with the strength of their ancestors and the spirits around them.

The young men of the Powhatan people of Virginia, in the north-eastern United States – a part of the Algonquin nation – were taken to a sacred area and dosed with a hallucinogenic plant medicine they called wysoccan for up to twenty days straight. The plant medicine was derived from jimson weed, a species of datura, which is a dangerous and very potent psychoactive plant – a member of the nightshade family. This near month-long experience was said to remove all memories of childhood. In the past it was reported that many youths didn't survive the ordeal. Those that did were marked with incredible strength for doing so.

When I went to visit the animist Iwol tribe in Senegal in 2016, I asked an elder of the community what initiations they put their young men through. He kept many of the details close to his chest, but explained that their twelve-to-thirteen-year-old boys would run through the village all day every day for a month, running in a traditional straight line, and then they would spend five months in the bush alone – fending for themselves and only returning after those five months were over.

In the Sateré-Mawé tribe of the Brazilian Amazon, in order to become men, youths must put their hands inside wicker mittens woven together with local plant fibres. These mittens are full of bullet ants. If you are not familiar with the bullet ant, there is a pain scale, called the Schmidt sting pain index, which goes from 1–4. This scale classes a sting from a bullet ant as a '4+ pain level' – the highest in the world. When stung in the foot – the usual place for an accidental encounter – one is said to feel a 'pure, intense, brilliant pain. Like walking over flaming charcoal with a three-inch nail embedded in your heel.' I can only imagine the sheer agony of this initiation.

These rites of passage are incredibly brutal, but they are not randomised acts of torture to the tribes that utilise them.

To them, they are spiritual and psychological means of transitioning children to adults while imbuing them with the correct qualities needed to protect their culture and tribe. To the tribes, the brutal nature of these initiations provides a ritualised type of violence that is needed to cause a fracture in the psyche of the initiate. This creates a wound large enough to break their identity so that they can be moulded into something new. It is through the testing nature of these rites of passage that the initiates are blown wide open and exposed to the transformational energies of their culture and environment, and are guided – through ritual – to remould and reshape themselves into somebody hard and resilient enough to support their community. These traditional cultures live from year to year and they do not have the resources to carry any passengers – which is a large reason why the initiations are non-negotiable. The youth simply must become useful, and the intense heat of the process of initiation makes sure that they are forged into that.

I believe traditional cultures are very smart to build solid and secure rites of passage that ensure this process occurs in the correct way. Their communities are generally a much tighter knit group than ours in the West and, due to this, as children they are more reliant on their community rather than one of two main caregivers. Part of the reason that the rites of passage are so testing is to shatter the illusion that life is always safe, and the childhood naivety that the community, and local surroundings, will always provide what they need. While this may have been the case when they were young, they eventually get to the age where they must transition from protected receiver to provider and protector, and a firm introduction to adulthood is needed to develop the necessary qualities to do this. But in the absence of these cultural rites of passage in the West, we still must face initiation – which is a natural process of growth. The difference between us and them is that our healing and initiation journeys are more individual and not sparked in a ritualised manner (although they can often be resolved with ritual later on). Our personal initiations are often sparked by a different sort of violence – trauma. Lack of empathy and presence, neglect, abuse, shocking incidents or the divorce of our caregivers are all scenarios that can cause a split and fracture in the previously healthy psyche of an individual. Therefore, similarly to our indigenous cousins – it is pain, and fear, that leads us into the initiatory journey.

Transitional periods in life often cause the pain of traumatic scenarios to resurface and push one into making a choice around transformation. Going to university and having to fend for yourself, or becoming a parent and feeling the weight of new responsibilities, can be overwhelming. Even starting a new job can bring up prior emotions of deep inadequacy and fear of change. Traditional initiation teaches us a valuable lesson and offers an important perspective, which is that pain is not something that needs to destroy us, but something that can actually be the starting point of a very empowering journey. This is not meant to minimise the seriousness of trauma or pain, but rather to look at it with a different attitude. Facing our individual pain may very well be the biggest test we experience in life. For many of us, our healing journey means facing the very thing we are most afraid of. Metaphorically, when we experience severance it can feel like we are confronting our own personal dragon. But it is worth remembering that dragons guard gold, and that gold is yours to claim.

To do so, however, we must enter the castle, into the chaos of the liminal.

Stage Two of Healing: Liminality

Liminality brings with it many sacred and transformative energies. Some psychoanalysts call the energies that we meet at this stage of our journey 'archetypes' – great and eternal patterns of human behaviour that inform how humans act in certain times during their life. Some traditional cultures believe that it is within the liminal stage that the spirits of that culture take hold of a person and reshape them, imbuing great power in them in the process. Either way, when we move into the liminal – the realm of our wounds and fears – we gain access to a sacred way of being and connect with the great power of soul.

This can be a difficult concept to get our heads around,

because despite the popularity of spirituality today, there is still not a cultural understanding in the West of what it feels like to be in touch with something sacred. A shaman from Mongolia once told me that we do not even have the correct language in the West for something as powerful and special as the soul, let alone the correct concepts for the various spirit types that inhabit the world around us. Therefore when we do meet with something truly sacred, either within us or externally, it can be a discombobulating experience as our current perception cannot compute it. What we do not understand, we usually fear, or disregard. This is nobody's fault, but a result of a cultural blind spot in our conceptual awareness due to our upbringing. The response to this fear and/or confusion is to analyse. But to analyse something that seems so illogical and irrational is a very difficult thing to do, particularly when we lack the cultural capacity to do so. It is like using a calculator to write a poem. Nevertheless, our mind uses whatever material it can in an attempt to understand just what the hell is going on, drawing symbols from our personal and cultural past, becoming more and more stimulated until it wears itself out and life starts to feel overwhelming.

This is where the mind's activity may seem as though it goes into overdrive. We may suffer huge delusions or intrusive thoughts, or become completely numb and disengaged with life. The difficulty at this stage lies in learning how to disidentify with these huge energies and stimuli and take what we are feeling much less personally. Instead, we must cultivate the courage to hand ourselves over to the energies beyond the current capacity of our minds, and trust that they will (eventually) leave us standing the right way up. To do this alone is incredibly frightening, so it is very helpful to seek out a guide who has completed this process themselves and is therefore able to guide you through it. My recommendation if you feel that you are in this stage of your healing process is to find an authentic healer who is connected to a lineage. This could be shamanic, animist, Buddhist or otherwise – as long as their lineage is authentic. They will be able to guide you through this delicate part of the journey and offer you guidance and techniques on how you can disidentify from the chaotic parts of your mind and surrender to your process. These techniques could be certain daily meditations, regular rituals, prayers or offerings (which will be discussed later in the book) or traditional herbs and medications. Sometimes a more urgent level of help is needed and a well-trained practitioner will need to perform a ceremony for you. Sacred space within a ceremony is also a liminal space, where the 'usual' rules for life don't apply. This is because the space becomes filled with very powerful energies in order to shift and shape a person who has become unbalanced in some way. If this is not possible for you, a well-regarded psychotherapist can provide excellent guidance.

In traditional cultures, all of this guidance would be provided by 'ritual elders' who have mapped this liminal stage and understand both the obstacles and the monumental energies that one might encounter. They are the ones that lead the traditional initiations and make sure that the initiates 'cook' properly within them.

If we lack a guide, in my experience two things tend to happen inside the liminal. One is that we feel as though the energies we encounter want to consume us. It can feel as though we are being swallowed and that the dark forces of the world are trying to break us down. We then fight against them – creating huge fear and paranoia as we slowly start to feel that if we stop resisting for even a moment then we will lose ourselves completely. We can put so much energy and focus into this resistance that it leads to a lot of dissociative-like symptoms as we develop tunnel vision and disconnect from the world around us, or dream up a fantasy world (often unconsciously) and seek to exist there instead. Although these forces do indeed want to break you down, they will only burn away what you are not. A spiritual crisis may emerge as we attempt to navigate a great sense of internal upheaval, which naturally leaks out into our external environment. A person may become unable to work their job, or to function in social situations. They may isolate themselves from life and become more and more identified with this deep sense of fragility. It is possible that a person becomes plagued with negative or intrusive thoughts around destruction and death. Tragically, in some cases, this may lead to suicide, as a person identifies completely with the parts of themselves that have come to the end of their life. This must be seen as a psychospiritual death instead of a literal one. Although part of a person does need to be laid to rest, this is only so that a deeper form of soul can emerge and take over.

Something else that may occur here is that people really enjoy these grandiose energies and identify with them completely. They may believe that they really are the 'archetypes' themselves. Quite commonly, this manifests in archetypal cultural figures such as King Arthur, Cleopatra, Jesus Christ or Buddha. Attached to this is a relentless and sometimes psychopathic sense of purpose. This can lead to huge amounts of grandiosity and dangerous situations as people may start to believe that, because they are these forces, they have access to supernatural amounts of power. They may believe they can fly and jump off buildings, or become utterly convinced their sole purpose is to liberate others from suffering and destroy the 'evil' forces of the world – waging war on innocent people they are convinced represent them. They may leave or even abuse their family dynamic to pursue 'otherworldly' goals – leaving a trail of family destruction in their wake. They may take superhuman amounts of drugs, or have superhuman amounts of sex, both of which start to consume them and eventually lead them to losing their grip on reality completely.

Although these are extreme examples and many more minor situations can occur between these two poles, on either end of the scale we can become stuck in the liminal for many years. It is a confusing, chaotic and disorienting process, which is why it is so important to find a personal 'ritual elder' who is able to lead us out of the liminal maze and back into the world. If you feel as though you are struggling with any of the above symptoms, I highly recommend speaking to somebody and receiving the help that you require. We must begin to remove the taboo and stigma around our psychological health, and while these can be normal processes for us all to go through at times in our lives, at their extremes they are debilitating and incredibly difficult to navigate.

Upon receiving the necessary guidance and assistance, I am certain that many are able to return to balance, reconnected with a new sense of purpose and with a stronger sense of self that has been forged through the fires of learning how to navigate their personal fears and obstacles.

Stage Three of Healing: Aggregation

We may have a few scars at this point, but as mythologist Martin Shaw once reminded me in one of his epic storytellings, 'It is okay to walk with a limp.' At this stage it can seem as if somebody has suddenly turned the lights back on. The show is over, and it is time to get yourself back in the world. The huge and boiling liminal energies have simmered down into something manageable and things that brought us so much fear, or so much confusion, suddenly seem crystal clear and controllable. This is true integration – the re-organisation of the psyche and absorption and acceptance of the previously misunderstood parts of ourselves so that we are able to choose to navigate the world with a much more full repertoire of human emotion. Pain may remain, and suffering is present, but through the inner journey you have undertaken you have proven to yourself that you are capable of rising to meet it. This is an important concept around healing. Your pain and suffering might not disappear completely, but the goal is to grow your awareness to the level that it seems much smaller than it used to be.

With this, an unshakeable confidence starts to permeate your decision-making, and a sense of clarity leads you through life. Although we may undertake this process many small times within our lives, it is when these larger journeys occur that we experience a true and lasting inner change.

As alluded to before, this journey often humbles a person, and creates a deep compassion. If you have ever escaped a situation by the skin of your teeth, you may know what I am talking about. 'Be proud, but do not remind the world of your deeds' are the apt words from an old West African song. When aggregated you gain access to a deep jewel of wisdom, one that you realise you had all along, but had to, in some way, earn the access to. You will often find that it is nearly impossible to explain the intricacies of your personal journey to somebody else with the same magnitude that you experienced it.

I spent many years stuck in the liminal, and it was only through finding shamanism that I was able to slowly come back to who I was and feel part of the world again. I was hugely fearful of my mind and the powerful and fierce liminal energies that seemed to play havoc with it, and it was the practice of shamanism that gave me the structure that I needed to understand how to work with them, and gave me access to the elder figures that I needed, at the right time in my life. Undertaking my own healing process gave me a renewed sense of meaning, which is so important during any big life shift. But underneath the intricacies of daily practice and psychological healing, the core of my healing journey really began when I was reconnected to the earth, something that to a young man from London seemed completely alien. This connection greatly assisted me in staying anchored during the liminal so that the great powers around me could release and transmute the strong energies of fear, anxiety and panic that had been stored in my body for so long.

Below is an account of one of the many initiations during my journey, for one of my trainings in core shamanism, a Western form of shamanism that was created by Michael Harner in the 1980s. It was a burial ceremony that had been inspired by indigenous cultures in Central America. This ceremony was incredibly powerful for me, and, as I lay buried in my grave in the womb-like earth, I was offered a ritual opportunity to be reborn. It was a true turning point for me in my life. While my own initiatory journey had been going on for a couple of years prior, this was a micro-initiation within the macro-initiation, a circle within a circle, and it really helped me in understanding, perhaps for the first time, that I was going to be okay.

We had spent the last two days digging our graves, and the sight of fourteen of them in the clay amongst the trees was a little disconcerting, to be honest. Even though we knew we were doing this ceremonially, it was hard not to tune into the collective terror shared by those who had, at some point in history, been forced to dig their own graves and get sealed inside them – dead or alive. Some participants, particularly those of Jewish Eastern European descent, wailed uncontrollably as their ancestral wounds bubbled to the surface.

We had been assured it was safe, and apparently there would be enough oxygen in each grave to last at least two days. We would only be sealed inside for around fourteen hours – which gave us plenty of time. Despite this, we had been asked to – as Western as it gets – sign a waiver that would relinquish our guides of responsibility were we to actually die. I tried not to think about that being a possibility. This burial ceremony was the last initiation of the first cycle of a core shamanic training, and we had proven our strength in three other initiations. It was time to practise what we had learnt, and to test the power of our minds.

One by one our teacher led us to the graves. We had spent the last few hours drumming by the fire and had all fallen into a collective trance. There was a misty aura around the ancient Sussex woodland, and the screech of tawny owls filled the air. When it came to be my turn, he motioned towards my grave.

As I climbed inside and lay on the cold, hard clay, I crossed my arms over my chest and took some deep breaths as the shaman's assistants lay sticks over the opening in the ground, sealing me in like a wooden cage, and then laid a tarp over them.

Thud, thud, thud. The sound of the heavy earth being piled on top of the tarp was deafening. It jolted me back into normal consciousness and into high alert, my heart bouncing out of my chest. The reality of what I was doing arrived with a panic, and I winced and tensed up as the stick roof bent and moaned under the weight of the earth. Slowly the light from the fire dimmed and I was left in pitch-black silence, lying alone in my ritual tomb, trying to calm my breath.

I lay there waiting for my eyes to adjust to the darkness, unsure of what to do next. We hadn't been instructed what to do once we were underground. With the prospect of countless hours with nothing to distract me, my mind started to analyse the situation.

Should I try to fall asleep? Meditate? Go into a trance? How would lying underground give me any healing anyway? Would something magic happen at some point during the night?

I had known this particular initiation was coming, and being quite claustrophobic I was dreading it. To my surprise, after some time I started to feel a sense of peace. I seemed to have slowly adjusted to the terror and it felt as though something was in the grave with me. Not in a spooky way, but a comforting one. It was something familiar. A warm sensation arose within me, and before long there was a complete absence of fear. I felt held by the earth, and in many ways safer than I had ever been. Whatever could possibly happen in the outside world over the next twelve or so hours couldn't affect me. I thought, even if a nuclear bomb went off, I would be safe in my little cocoon.

We had been preparing for this initiation for months, and a while back I had experienced a vision of a white flower. In that vision I entered the flower through its ovary, and underneath it was my mother's womb. Inside the womb, I saw myself as a baby. I felt her intense anxiety at the time, her deep uncertainty about how her life would play out, and if she was going to be able to give me the life she wanted. I felt her extreme sadness and worry. I also recognised that same anxiety and uncertainty about the world in myself, and the extreme sadness and worry that I had felt throughout my life. While this vision was showing me the interconnectedness between my mother's pain and mine, it also showed me that it was the severance between my mother and the earth that had caused this anxiety and worry. Like so many in Western cultures, she had experienced her own absence of holding. In the vision the flower petals started to drop one by one as the worry and pain became too much. Cut off from the nourishing earth, the flower began to wilt, as it could not draw nutrients from the land that supported it. The life and the vibrancy fell away and the flower could no longer support the creation of something beautiful. In the vision I came out of the flower crooked, hunched over and worried. I remembered this vision in the grave, and emotion overcame me. Not sadness, but awe. Awe at what mothers go through when creating life, and awe at the inter-connectedness of existence. As I closed my eyes and was once again overtaken by the vision state, I started to stand up tall as the flower once again regained its strength. I looked up at the world, free and supported by a sense of inner peace and confidence.

As I lay in the earth that night, my earth mother – the mother that we all share – nourished me in the way that I'd needed as an unborn child but had been unable to be due to the life circumstances of my mother – which were abso-lutely out of her hands. Ritually I was inside the womb again, and the pain of my past was being soothed. I was being given a second chance through the ritual.

By the time the morning came, and they dug me out again, I didn't want to leave.

This example of separating from the story of our biological mother and reconnecting with the earth mother is a common initiatory vision. It symbolises the forming of a strong sense of individuality, and a reconnection and sense of belonging to the earth. All of us, at some point, must go through this process in some way if we are to connect to our true potential. It allowed me to grow into an adult, and become somebody who could support my mother in her life, instead of depending on her for my own emotional stability. I arrived in the grave as a son, and I emerged from it a man.

RITUAL 1

Creating an Altar

An altar is a sacred place. For thousands of years humans have created altars to make offerings, to pray, and to connect with higher powers. An altar is sacred technology that acts as a sort of 'portal' that helps us connect from our world to the otherworlds. Much of a shaman's work is done in front of their altar, which gains huge amounts of energy and power over time.

While this ritual is not designed to create a working shamanic altar, as this takes many initiations and years of training, it will allow you to create a sacred place in your home where you can pray, meditate and collect protective energy for you and your loved ones.

There are thousands of different altars from around the world and they are all set up in slightly different ways according to the culture that they represent. They are often complex and include symbolism that relates to their local tradition. This is a very simple design that anybody can set up, which includes representations of the four elements of nature and items that have personal meaning to you.

Earth - Fire - Water - Air

(You can use different elemental representations if you like; these are just guidelines.)

WHAT YOU NEED

- A table (30cm x 30cm minimum)
- An object that represents fire – candle/figure
- An object that represents water – cup/shell

- An object that represents air - feather/flag
- An object that represents earth - rock/ crystal
- Sacred herbs or resins - juniper/mugwort/ sage/palo santo/frankinsence/copal
- Any items that have meaning for you - photographs of ancestors/sacred jewellery, etc
- Any items you wish to empower with sacred intention - a journal/diary
- Any items that represent things you would like to call into your life - coins/ notes for financial stability/a small bowl of fruit for abundance

It is important to only use ethically and responsibly sourced materials, and do not take objects from nature without first reading Chapter 7 on offerings.

CREATING AND MAINTAINING THE ALTAR

- Choose a place in your home that is free from clutter, and where natural light shines.

- Clean the table with a small mixture of warm water and citrus juice.
- Once the table is clean, place your objects on the altar, creating a border, and clean them with the smoke of the ethically sourced sacred herbs or resins. You can do this by moving the smoke in a clockwise direction, or by fanning the smoke with an ethically sourced feather, or gently blowing.
- Place the other items in the space in the centre.
- If you have a cup – replace the water with clean water each time you pray or sit with your altar (natural spring water is best). Empty this into nature after one day (leaving an empty cup is okay).
- Do not let fruit spoil, but eat it or place it in nature after one or two days – replacing it with new fruit.
- An altar is a responsibility, and how we keep our altar represents our intention for our lives. Keep it clean and never place anything on the altar that is not sacred.

CHAPTER 2

Spirituality as a Business – the New Age

Common mental disorders (CMDs) include different types of depression, anxieties, panic disorders, phobias and obsessive-compulsive disorders. Since 1993, in the UK, the prevalence of CMDs has risen by 20 per cent in both men and women. One in four people now admit they are suffering from some kind of mental health issue, and this huge increase doesn't show any sign of slowing down. This figure doesn't even take into account increasingly common issues such as bipolar, psychotic disorders and PTSD. It is not just adults who are affected either. In young people the figures are largely the same, with one in six children experiencing some kind of mental health disturbance. That is roughly six children in each classroom. To make things worse – for both adults and children – these figures don't include those who suffer from suicidal thoughts and self-harm, which do not constitute a diagnosable mental health condition, according to the NHS.

Suicide remains the biggest killer of young people ages five to nineteen, and of men under fifty.

Speaking to a Wixárika mara'akame (shaman) in Wales, he explained that one reason for this sharp rise in psychological issues is that, as a culture, we have lost our spiritual symbols, which help to provide us meaning and psychological security. In the past, these symbols acted as psychological safeguards and maps of meaning for those who believed in them. Looking at Britain's most popular religion in recent time, Christianity, the symbols of God or Jesus, although deities, are also symbols of the power that Christianity represents. Christians are able to orientate their psyche around these symbols to assist them in finding meaning in their life, despite hardship. These symbols also allow believers to feel that a higher power is watching over them, which is an especially beneficial belief when life does get tough, as it gives them the confidence that there is a higher wisdom to their struggle (we will explore the benefits of meaning and struggle later in the book), and that something powerful has their back in the face of adversity. The symbols in each religion provide us with what psychologists may call 'external unifying centres'. These are external mirrors that we can base our internal psychological structure on, which informs our behaviour, morality and thought processes. Having a strong external unifying centre helps us anchor to a feeling of psychological safety when life becomes chaotic. All religions provide, amongst other things, these external unifying centres, which help us function in healthy ways. Prayer directed at these symbols allows us to feel like we are taking a weight off our shoulders, and communal or individual ceremony that honours these symbols allows us to heal and renew ourselves. At its best, a religion provides firm structure for a community, and a common theme of belief that provides guidelines for that community's morality and behaviours – which can then, generally, all be in line with each other. What must also be said is that if you fall outside of the moral guidelines of a religion, this can have the opposite effect. When a religion is weaponised, it almost always leads to devastating and tragic results. All religions have their faults, but the fact remains that in the past, for many, they provided a certain psychological security that all human cultures throughout time has had – apart from ours during the last fifty years.

Recent censuses show that the UK is now one of the least religious countries in the world, and from 2011 to 2021 the number of people who identify with 'no religion' has increased by eight million. It seems that perhaps these monotheistic religions no longer represent the views of many of those who exist in the modern world. So much so that, in the same study, the 'non-religious' surged by almost 60 per cent. This is a huge shift in the spiritual dynamics of the country. It may be fair to say that these former bastions of belief have had their day. The average person, for whatever reason, is becoming less and less interested in them.

But I wonder, if we overlay the upward trend of mental health issues with the downward trend of religion in the UK, would we come to the same conclusion as the Wixárika healer? That the mental health crisis is indeed, in part, due to a loss of spiritual belonging and meaning in the West.

Many people are now coming to understand that although the power of mainstream religions is beginning to fade, their inherent human need for meaning has not gone anywhere. In fact, referring once again to the rising trend in mental health statistics, it is highly likely that our need for meaning in life has increased. People are coming to realise that something is not as it should be, they want to know why they are here, why they are suffering and how they can heal, and it is within this great search that I feel more and more people are turning to alternative forms of spirituality. The yoga, meditation and spiritual industry is booming, and wellness is widely seen to be the latest trend. TikTok, Instagram and X are awash with spiritual influencers and it is now 'cool to be conscious'. This is, by all means, an absolutely wonderful thing. Young people are becoming more aware and are searching for answers. The hunger for spiritual meaning is real, but in the midst of this hunger, we must remember that the most important thing is education. When I began on my spiritual journey I had no guide as to what was authentic and what wasn't. Due to this, I found myself down many dead-ends, sometimes even hurting myself in the process and feeling worse off than I was before.

This chapter is about learning to navigate the Western spiritual culture – often called the New Age. There is a polite criticism of its core concepts, and a suggestion of how, instead, we would be better off to humbly look to the tried and tested practices of ancient lineages and the spirituality that they offer for a grounded, slower and more realistic expectation to healing, as well as their authentic concepts of morality and compassion that can greatly impact how we feel about ourselves and the world around us.

THE NEW AGE

It all began in the late nineteenth century. Helena Petrovna Blavatsky, a Russian mystic who moved to New York in 1875, co-founded the Theosophical Society – an organisational body for an esoteric religious movement, which borrowed ideas from Hindu and Buddhist ideologies, such as reincarnation and karma, and combined them with metaphysics and some Greek philosophy. The aim of the society was to usher in a new age for humanity and prepare us for the coming of what she called the World Teacher, who would help propel the world forward, ridding it of stigma, hate and all of the other mucky parts of humanity. She said she channelled this information from the ascended masters of the Great White Brotherhood – a race of white-cloaked beings of perfect nature and great power. Her successor, Annie Besant, a Freemason and theosophist, carried on Blavatsky's teachings and claimed the World Teacher that the earth had been waiting for was Jiddu Krishnamurti, who was 'discovered' and adopted by Besant as a 14-year-old. She raised him to be the World Teacher, and although he did become a famed spiritual figurehead and speaker, he eventually renounced his role and split from the Theosophical Society, denouncing it publicly.

Moving onward into the 1920s, a British philosopher and author, Alice Bailey, founded the Arcane School. Some say she is the first writer to coin the term 'New Age' officially, although this is hard to prove. She *also* claimed to channel an ascended master (are you noticing a trend?) – this time a deceased Tibetan teacher called Djwal Khul. He has never been proven to have existed, but according to American New Age teacher Elizabeth Clare Prophet, he was a reincarnation of Caspar, one of the Three Wise Men who visited the baby Jesus. Alice Bailey followed her predecessor Blavatsky, and borrowed the identity of *her* future messiah from an authentic tradition – Buddhism – citing the future Buddha Lord Maitreya as the spiritual master that the world was waiting for. After Bailey's death in 1949 the movement rolled on. In 1971, American philosopher, and self-appointed practical mystic, David Spangler further developed the core ideas around what we know as the New

Age movement, in his book *Revelation: The Birth of a New Age*. This time, he channelled a different spirit, named John. It was during this time that the New Age merged with the hippie-psychedelic movement, and psychedelic advocates such as psychologists Timothy Leary and Richard Alpert (more widely known as Baba Ram Dass) combined ideas they had learnt from Eastern mysticism with more Western psychology, this time infused with the psychedelic experience (although Alpert did move towards the more traditional spiritual path in later years). It was here that the New Age further absorbed countercultural ideologies, spurred on by its new alliance with the anti-establishment psychedelic movement, and gained huge popularity in the West due to the outrage and political unrest over the Vietnam War.

The New Age evolved in this time to focus on two fundamental beliefs. One was that the New Age was always just around the corner, and that, when it did arrive, it would rid the world of suffering and pain. The other was that, in order to not get left behind when it did finally arrive, humans needed to develop themselves spiritually. The tools to aid this transformation were borrowed from thousand-year-old spiritual traditions, such as Buddhism, shamanism, animism and Hinduism, but taken out of their original context, diluted and mishmashed together. Psychedelics and Western forms of transpersonal psychology via Jung and Assagioli were infused into this mishmash, alongside stoicism and gnostic teachings, crytals, channelling, ceremonial magick and other occult practices. The New Age movement continues to evolve to this day, where alternative spirituality is arguably more popular than ever amongst the mainstream. With more and more spotlights being shone on these practices, many business-minded folk have seen an opportunity to get involved within an unregulated industry and satiate the hunger for wellness and spiritual meaning that exists in the West. With the invention and evolution of the internet and social media, the New Age has become a huge business – an online marketplace where a Westerner can access all of the world's spirituality woven into one package. With innocent roots in counterculture and the expansion of conscious-ness, the fabric of the New Age has now become firmly woven into the capitalist tapestry. In the need to outdo each other it is popular to combine many practices together, to get people through the door and sell as many products as possible. Adverts for shamanic Reiki, tantric cacao aya-huasca ceremonies and Celtic kirtans are just a few of the examples I found when researching this book. These prac-tices were never combined together in their original traditional settings and many of them are from completely different traditions from different parts of the world. The issue is that the merging of two different practices often brings in conflicting energies that can have negative conse-quences. Because of this, the New Age, while meaning well, has unfortunately become Frankenstein's monster sitting in a lotus position.

But it is where I, and many others, began their exploration into spirituality, and I am thankful for that. As a bright-eyed young man from London, incredibly eager to develop my spiritual practice, I devoured as many workshops, training courses and events as I could. It was an incredibly exciting time, because the New Age told me that nothing was as it seemed, and that anything I previously knew about the world was false. It promised me the possibility that anything could be real and opened me up to a world that seemingly had no limits. My previously narrow worldview expanded and, before long, I started to feel the desire to leave my original friendship circles because of their insistence on what I believed to be boring and small-minded logic.

My reasoning for this was because I aligned with the big intention that binds all of the sewn-together practices of the New Age, which is to ascend past your human troubles and complete a transformation into pure light. It was in this light that all your problems – ego, sickness or otherwise – would cease to exist. Life would be perfect. At the time, that was music to my ears, and after nearly fifteen years of suffering I flew straight towards it like a moth to a flame.

But, like a moth to a flame, instead of reaching nirvana, I burnt myself. For what is so conveniently omitted in these surface-level New Age practices is the fact that in order to transform into light we must all face, and accept, our own inner darkness. Instead of doing this, in the New Age circles that I became part of we were often instructed to bypass the dark and uncomfortable emotions inside of us completely. Sometimes we were taught this directly, but sometimes it was shown to us indirectly by the teachers and supposed gurus who would only show us their smiles and preach superficial wisdom that didn't help us much in the real world. Any form of conflict was considered taboo. Slowly, as I got more involved in these communities, I started to hear whispers and rumours amongst students that these same teachers and gurus were actually committing acts of abuse behind the scenes. So much dedication had been given to these teachers, creating such a powerful bond between student and teacher, that some students refused to believe it. The brave students that did come out and say something were ostracised from the group and accused of crying wolf or being jealous. Unfortunately, the truth is that many modern gurus have been proven to have abused their power, or been shown to have taken advantage of their students' trust and vulnerability. A tantra teacher of mine was arrested for sexual assault shortly after I had paid thousands of pounds to go and study with him abroad. This isn't an isolated incident, with many well-known Western tantra teachers being arrested at some point in their careers. In fact, it took me a while to learn that what these teachers were teaching was not tantra at all. Tantra is an ancient, incredibly respected and effective system of practice that is handed down, often in secret, from teacher to student. It is a hardcore practice and while sex is included in the practice in certain, very specific situations, it is not the focus at all.

There is an assumption in Western New Age spirituality that a guru or healer must be somewhat enlightened – especially a well-known one. Due to this, a person who attends a workshop, retreat or a healing session may be tempted to remove many of their normal boundaries as they hand themselves over to the practitioner to 'fix' them. If their pain is great enough, and the faith strong enough in the healer or the practice, many will do whatever it takes to heal – including going along with situations that they would never normally comply with in their normal life. A dangerous combination can arise, where the healer can do whatever they want without anybody checking their behaviour, and the client goes along with it because they believe it is part of their healing process.

I encourage people to understand that whenever power dynamics are at play, the opportunity for abuse can arise. Abuse is much less likely when two people feel equal in their power. Spirituality – in the context of the teacher and student relationship, or healer and client dynamic – is inherently unbalanced. Much care must be taken when finding a teacher and healer.

Earth-centric cultures help to prevent abuse by appointing an assembly of wise and trusted elders, who are well placed to counsel and recognise harmful behaviours before they are acted out. They have seen everything before, and as the Kikuyu people of Kenya say, 'An old man sitting on a stool can see further than a young man who has climbed a tree.' Because it is such a new spiritual culture, with no lineage, this old and integrated wisdom is lacking in the New Age. The West will eventually have these elders, but, until that point comes, there are not many people who practise spirituality outside of traditional contexts that have anyone monitoring their behaviour, who has 'been there, done that, got the T-shirt'. This can lead to the innate power dynamics of teacher/student and healer/seeker becoming too unbalanced and leading to harm.

Western psychotherapist and founder of analytical psychology Carl Jung famously said:

One does not become enlightened by imagining figures of light, but by making the darkness conscious.

What he meant by this is that for each of us to grow and heal we must first learn how to bring awareness to all of the parts of us that we do not want to show the world. This includes all of the destructive, distasteful and potentially monstrous aspects of our personality. There is an irony in this, as many of us begin our healing journeys to get as far as we can from these parts of ourselves!

In part, this was why the New Age was originally so tempting for me. The opportunity to heal all my issues without ever having to suffer the humiliation of admitting my weaknesses was one that seemed too good to pass up. Unfortunately, it is just a fantasy, which led to more suffering – without having a relationship with our darkness, we fail to notice when our darkness is driving our behaviours. The glaring issue with the New Age is that the overfocus on ascending our humanity, and the supposed chanelling of ascended masters, is too unbalanced. This is where I became drawn to the practice of shamanism, as it provided a grounded spiritual approach that welcomed all of me, not just the parts that aligned with love and light.

BUILDING A RELATIONSHIP WITH DARKNESS

In my personal journey within the New Age I didn't ever feel as if anger, jealousy, aggression or desire were welcome. Although I *felt* these emotions, I didn't want anyone to know it for fear of rejection, so I pushed them down and suppressed them, acting like they weren't there. I was not taught that each time we suppress emotion our internal pressure builds. Emotions come with energetic charges.

Both science and spirituality agree that since energy cannot be destroyed, it always goes somewhere. When we suppress our emotions, the energy of them is stored in both the body and our psyche. We may be able to do this for years, until eventually, often quite spontaneously, the pressure becomes too much and a huge outpouring of emotion erupts, causing havoc. This is a common occurrence all over our culture, as people suppress more and more only to develop incredibly short fuses, which end up causing them and others huge amounts of distress when they finally burst. This 'bursting' is not always an outward reaction, it can also manifest internally as psychological issues such as intrusive thoughts or violent fantasies, which can be (though not always) exaggerated messages from the unconscious parts of our psyche that are signalling to us that we need to release or integrate our emotions.

In 2018 I ran men's groups from a retreat centre in Bedfordshire, where I introduced men to shamanic concepts and ceremony. One of the most common themes in men who would come was that they had been silent for too long about how they really felt. Often this was because they felt they had nobody to talk to, or felt as if they would lose their masculinity if they showed themselves being vulnerable. But sometimes it was simply because they didn't have the language or awareness about how they felt, so were unable to express and release it. They knew something was wrong, but didn't know what it was, or how to voice it. All they could conclude was that something was 'off'. I come from a background of this sort of male behaviour and recognise it well. While I have full respect for the working man being tough and 'getting on with it', this can lead to complications if you don't have a healthy way of regulating your stress as it inevitably builds. Each person can do this in their own way. For some it is meditation, for others exercise or a cold beer with friends after work. What is important is that each of us makes space to decompress without too much distraction. My tension had always been there, but the overemphasis on purity in the New Age community made it much worse. I had spent the last few years doing spiritual work, but I had focussed too much on ascending upward, instead of rooting down into the earth, exploring my emotions and grounding myself. Eventually, this became too much, and, for me, it was discovering the sweat rituals from around the world that played a huge part in the release of years of built-up tension.

Sweat Rituals

A sweat lodge is an animist practice, also called a ceremonial sauna. Many cultures from around the world have some sort of a sweat ritual. Indigenous traditions from Scandinavia, the Mediterranean, Japan, the Middle East and North and Central America all partake in a ritual sauna to purify their bodies and minds, heal from illness, pacify their thoughts and honour the local spirits. The 'sweat' is an ancient and simple ceremony that combines the elements – fire, water, earth and air – inside a sacred space. The fire heats the rocks (earth), which are taken into a structure where water is poured onto them. This creates steam (air). Ritually combining the elements of creation creates a potent container for ceremony in which to pray, let go of tension and surrender to the searing heat, which causes a person to sweat intensely, purifying both their body and mind.

A well-held sweat ceremony can facilitate a huge release of emotional charge, which allows someone to let go of huge amounts of the stuck and pressurised energy that they have accumulated. Periodically we all need this, as life is stressful, and in traditional cultures this is sometimes called 'staying clean'. These cultures understand that all people build up huge emotional backlogs of stress from the goings on in life, and know that if this builds up too much then the community will be affected by the spontaneous and uncontrolled release that inevitably follows. The distress caused by holding in too much emotion without expressing it can also cause huge amounts of tension in the body of the individual, which can lead to various diseases of the body and mind. While there are other reasons for a sweat ritual – including birth and death ceremonies – community sweat rituals often take place so that people can feel more emotionally regulated and refreshed.

A big part of these community sweat rituals is prayer. Prayer is often broken up into two parts. One is to honour powers greater than ourselves and our ancestors, and the other is asking for help. The ceremonial sauna on our men's retreats would take place on Saturday evening after two days of intense psychological and spiritual work. We did it this way so that we were able to gently bring a lot of their 'stuff' to the surface. By the time Saturday evening came, and we had fasted and danced around a fire together for hours and hours, men would often be moved to tears by just admitting out loud to other men within the sauna that they were hurting deeply inside. Inside the ceremonial sweat it is pitch black, searingly hot and very uncomfortable. Nervousness and apprehension often disappear. When sitting together naked on the cool muddy earth, people usually lose some of their inhibitions and find it easier to be honest. This gives the opportunity for these men to open up emotionally with intention and be received, sometimes for the very first time. It is an incredibly moving experience, and the ritual space allowed each man to finally start to let go of burdens that they had been carrying alone for so long, and also witness and receive other men doing the same. This allows the healing to go two ways, and by the end of it we would have twenty-five sweaty and muddy men – bonded for life – who left the sauna a lot lighter than they'd arrived.

As community-based creatures, being seen and received for our honesty and vulnerability is a very rewarding and nourishing thing, and it naturally compels us to want to do the same for others. Slowly but surely, this creates a domino effect of honesty and acceptance that cuts off shame from its roots, allowing people to bring back troubling emotions from the unconscious and integrate them into their wider personality. Something I love about shamanic ceremony is the honesty that it encourages. Although it can be terrifying to pray and open up and show others your weakest parts, this allows a redemption that is essential for humans who are looking to heal.

A potent way to escape the cycle of heavy burden and personal shame is the radical acceptance of darkness within humanity, and safe, ritualised spaces in which to explore it – such as those that shamanism provides. With access to these spaces, we can then begin to understand and integrate these parts of us so that they don't drive our behaviours from the unconscious parts of our psyche. Alongside this, we must be compassionate enough to offer redemption to ourselves, and others, so that we can renew and grow into more rounded individuals.

In order to heal we must come to accept the parts of us that we hide from the world. In doing this we learn to understand them, gaining a deeper level of awareness of how we act and why we do what we do. This is the goal of self-realisation – to realise the vast components of the self and become in control of our emotions, actions and habits. Although the New Age was a wonderful starting point for me, and for many others, I do believe that the overfocus on love and light is a huge issue that leads to a lot of unnecessary harm. If Western spiritual culture is going to move forward, it would benefit from becoming inspired by the radical acceptance of traditional and indigenous cultures and inviting the darker sides of ourselves into sacred space so that we can work with them and show them compassion. This in turn teaches us to be compassionate with others, as when we accept the darkness that exists within us, we also accept it when we see it in other people. Getting our true humanity 'out on the table' removes a lot of the tension and secrecy behind the actions and behaviours that may lead to abuse – leading to a safer and more welcoming society.

RITUAL 2

Honouring the Directions

Throughout the process of healing it is incredibly important to stay grounded and connected to the earth. An amazing way to do this is to learn a simple ritual of 'honouring the directions'.

Honouring the directions is an effective way to ground yourself in the centre of life. Growing up in the West, we are often told that the world doesn't revolve around us. This may be true in an egoic sense, but in order to feel grounded it is important that we periodically centre ourselves in the middle of existence.

This short ritual can be performed as a simple but powerful exercise that starts to teach you how to orient yourself in the world and how important it is to feel grounded. The technique explained below is simple, and it should start to shift the sometimes chaotic world back into balance.

- Each morning when you wake up, go to your altar and spend some time cleaning it with sacred smoke, as instructed in the previous ritual.
- When you are done, take a deep breath and stand facing towards the north.
- With your right hand up, and your left hand resting on your heart, call to the

north: 'Great powers of the north. I honour and welcome you – I place myself at the centre of existence.'

- Turn to the west, raising your right hand again and keeping your left hand on your heart: 'Great powers of the west. I honour and welcome you – I place myself at the centre of existence.'
- Turn to the south, raising your right hand again and keeping your left hand on your heart: 'Great powers of the south. I honour and welcome you – I place myself at the centre of existence.'
- Turn to the east, raising your right hand again and keeping your left hand on your heart: 'Great powers of the east. I honour and welcome you – I place myself at the centre of existence.'
- If you have ancestors from a certain direction, or feel very connected to a place, you can add additional honourings to these directions.
- It is a useful addition for all of the rituals in this book to keep a shamanic journal

that you can document your experiences in. Over time this will help you notice your emotions and cycles, and assist you in feeling more grounded and connected to your practice.

CHAPTER 3

Taking Off the Rose-Tinted Glasses

When you think of shamanism, it may conjure up images of far-off rainforest villages, remote desert dwellings, wind-swept mountain ridges and long, rolling green steppes as far as the eye can see. When I first became interested in these practices it was partly for the exoticism and the escapism that came from reading anthropological accounts of ceremony and healing. I never once, in the earlier years, thought that what I was reading would ever apply to me personally. At this time I was working as a teaching assistant in a school for primary-aged children with special needs, and on my wage there was absolutely no way I could travel to these places. I felt pangs of sorrow when I looked around my own landscape of grey concrete – my interest in earth-centric spirituality could only exist in my imagination. This chapter is about my first forays into sha-manic practice, and how I became inspired to see my own culture through a shamanic lens. I include my early expe-riences with plant medicine and traditional cultures, and how we must be aware of our intentions when we feel drawn to work with them. All of this assisted in inspiring me to find genuine ways to start to integrate shamanic and earth-centric spiritualities into our culture so that we can balance and heal ourselves and, vitally, reconnect to our land.

I was thrilled whenever authentic traditions came to England as it gave me a chance to experience them first-hand without the long-distance travelling, which I simply couldn't afford to do. I had heard about a shamanic gathering in Cambridge, which was not far from where I grew up in North London. Elders from several cultures from around the world had come to partake in a four-day ritual that would both honour our land here, and also teach us Westerners about the correct way of going about ritual. Eagerly, I booked my ticket, hoping to meet with and learn from some of the healers from the traditions that I had read so much about. As I arrived and set up my tent, I spent the rest of the day observing the goings-on. It was my first time in a place like this, and it was a far cry from the usual surroundings of raves and festivals. As I took it all in, one of the first things I noticed was how normal and down-to-earth the elders and their entourages were, and how bizarrely over the top a lot of the Westerners were being. Healers who had grown up in the Amazon rainforest were wearing T-shirts and shorts and Oakley sunglasses, and many of the English people were the ones wearing feathers, huge amounts of traditional jewellery and ponchos. There also seemed to be a high level of psychedelic use amongst the English, although admittedly the substances were seen as sacred. Rapé was also being used by pretty much every single Westener. Rapé, or hapé, is a snuff mixture of ash, tobacco and herbs and is ritually used in ceremonies in the Amazon rainforest to purify the mind and body. It is blown up the nose with a pipe made from bamboo or animal bone, and it was being blasted up the noses of a lot of them, a lot of the time. Others were mixing other plant medicines like peyote and huachuma with magic mushrooms. There was one group of English people from the south who, to all appearances, constantly spoke and sang in Spanish. I interviewed a Colombian medicine man afterwards, and he remarked that he had been on the medicine path for many years, but whenever he went to the UK he heard English people singing Spanish medicine songs that he had never heard before. He, like I, was confused as to where our local sacred songs were, and if we had any in the first place.

With all this in mind, I left feeling torn. I had enjoyed my experience immensely and had learnt a great deal, but I could not help but feel that earth-centric forms of spirituality in the West would never take root if all we did was attempt to mimic other cultures. Instead, in my eyes, it felt more realistic to learn from them, and then, with their blessing, apply their methodology to our own lands. This way we could see earth-centric spiritual practice like a formula and then apply that formula in our own native tongue and with our own culture. For example, instead of singing songs about the condor and hummingbird, who have never been present on our land, could we learn the bones of the song and instead include the owl and crow, who live just outside our window? Could we replace the prayer for the jaguar with the red fox or lynx? As an observer, it was also hard to justify such a huge use of substances. In the traditional context many of these substances are treated with a reverence that is hard to comprehend as a Westerner, and we have very little in our culture that is of such elevated respect. Although people may *understand* the concept of a plant being sacred, I didn't feel as though many people were truly giving it the respect required. It seemed at times that many Westerners were treating the gathering as a psychedelic jolly – which didn't sit well with me at all.

The respect and reverence that is needed for these hugely powerful substances, and the spirits that they bring with them, is essential, as these are not plants to be trifled with. I often work with clients who have been burnt by a psychedelic medicine ceremony, which has been too much for them and they have been left unable to put themselves back together psychologically, feeling as though they have lost grip on reality. Whenever I've asked who held their ceremony, it is very, very rarely a healer from an indigenous culture. Usually it's a Westerner who has travelled to the Amazon for a few months, come back and self-proclaimed themselves a shaman, and has begun serving up the incredibly powerful medicines themselves without much, or any, training. It happens with many other plant medicines too, and it unfortunately puts a dark spin on a way of healing that can have miraculously wonderful effects.

I speak from experience as I have had wonderful but also negative plant medicine experiences. In my early twenties I travelled to the Netherlands for a week-long ayahuasca immersion, which also included fasting – which I had never done before. I had no idea what I was getting myself into and I had simply googled 'ayahuasca ceremony' while stoned in my flat in Clapton and chosen the second link that popped up. This is something that I do not recommend. When I arrived everyone was nice and seemed knowledgeable, but it is only looking back with hindsight that I realise they had very little experience. We had to sit in absolute silence most of the weekend – even outside of the ceremony. During the ceremonies they played indigenous ceremonial songs through a Bluetooth speaker from a Spotify playlist. The fasting was really difficult, as ayahuasca often leads to serious purging from both ends of the body. After a long night of this we were hardly allowed to eat anything to replenish our strength. I experienced a small breakdown after the week, and it made all of my mental health symptoms a lot worse for a long time. It wasn't healing at all, and was genuinely quite traumatic. It took me months to recover. At the time I thought this was just part of the process. A year or two later, I sat with an indigenous healer from Brazil, and the experience was completely different. I felt good throughout – despite puking my guts up as usual – and while it did take a little while to integrate the lessons that the ceremony taught me about myself, it was much more gentle than my week in the Netherlands. I have also experienced huge amounts of healing when I have sat with the Wixárika and taken their medicine – hikuri (peyote) – which I have done many times. So while there is, rightfully, a spotlight on the incredibly powerful healing benefits of sacred psychedelics (entheogens), it is helpful to understand that they are not silver bullets for healing and can also, in the wrong hands, go wrong. These medicines, and the spirits that accompany them, are incredibly powerful, and the issue is not in the medicine, which is wonderfully healing, but in the human capability for error. It takes many years of training to be able to create a safe space when working with these plants so that the spirits of the medicine can be correctly worked with and pacified if needed. A shaman must also be able to read a participant's energy to know how much of a dose they require. The only way to learn this is through sacrifice and time, and there are no shortcuts. The actual plant is just one part of the ceremony. The sacred songs that move and shift the energies throughout the night, and the deep and complex cosmologies that surround and support the use of these plants, are just as important. A traditional ayahuascero apprenticeship, for example, is very hardcore and takes over a decade, and a Wixárika healer told me that in order to serve peyote to the community they must first complete a series of 'charges', which each last five years and which prepare them in the various aspects needed to safely perform the all-night ritual for their community. If those who are born into these cultures train for upwards of a decade to perform these rituals safely, then it makes no sense to me how Westerners – visitors to these cultures – begin serving these same medicines after six months of experience, and feel they can do this in a safe way.

In my public talks, people are often surprised to hear that most shamanic cultures do not use psychedelic plants at all. In some traditions, the use of psychedelic medicines is even seen as taboo. Part of my original fascination with these medicines came from the ease with which I could have a mystical experience through ingestion of these plants and participating in the ceremonies. It is difficult to induce a spiritual trance by drumming, dancing, chanting or playing another instrument like a jaw harp or a bell, but it is easy to take a psychedelic medicine and have a spiritual experience. This opens it up for many people and, in the right circumstances, is extremely positive and life changing. There are incredibly encouraging studies for the use of psychedelic medicines in end-of-life care, and for those with intense PTSD. With the right practitioner and setting, there is no doubt that they can be therapeutic. In the wrong hands, however, they can be seriously problematic. But let us remember – all spirituality incurs risk. A person can suffer negative mental health issues from too much meditation, or from meditating for too long in the wrong way. Yoga, if practised the wrong way, can cause injury. We have already touched upon the issues with Western versions of tantra. Spirituality can be dangerous, and healing can be hardcore. The Western mind can be an incredibly fragile thing and it doesn't take much to affect it in an adverse way. This is why it is so essential to practise spirituality slowly, in an authentic way, with a good teacher who can keep you on track. There are many roads to the same place – but the path must be solid enough to get you there.

I was also drawn to these exotic cultures and psychedelic medicines because I held a belief that our life in the West was void of spiritual experience. Going back to my pangs of sorrow around my concrete surroundings, where the only bursts of vibrancy seemed to come from neon advertisements (I was a city boy after all, and this was before I had ever spent a meaningful amount of time in nature). I think that with this feeling of sorrow comes an intense feeling of hunger, a desire to travel to other parts of the world and immerse ourselves in another's culture. Innocently, in the West there is a glamour that surrounds spirituality. While this glamour is absent within the traditional cultures that I have spent time with, this Western outlook really feeds into our susceptibility for consumerism. We are often led by desire in the West, and our capitalist culture feeds off it. This naturally crosses over into our views on spirituality too – which are not separate from our culture – and those of us who are desperate for a more nourishing connection to the earth, and community, look at other cultures who have it and yearn for it for ourselves. This isn't malicious, but it comes from a place of lack. Sadly, though, in trying to fill a hole and soothe one of our primal cultural wounds – the separation from the divine – when we do arrive in these exotic places and experience their spiritual beauty, we want to bring a piece of it home with us and maybe even start giving people the experiences that we had. This seems to, in my experience, happen more often when psychedelics are involved, because we can experience the otherworlds and spirits so easily by ingesting them and feel we can assist others in doing the same. As we discussed in the first chapter about healing, in the liminal space, people can often succumb to delusions of grandeur, and this can manifest as believing that the spirits are telling them to bring their message to the modern world. Perhaps this is true, or maybe it is just projection, but either way we must remember that all too often, within this hazy lust of magic and ambition, we forget that these cultures have had to fight tooth and nail for the very survival of their traditions – usually fighting people who were from the West – and that by us coming over and taking back their culture to our own shores, and then repackaging it for a Western audience and making money from it, we are diluting their culture and inadvertently colonising them in another, more subtle way.

When I noticed this about myself, I realised that to rectify it I needed to start observing my own culture in a deeper way, to see where exactly the apparent separation between what is spiritual and what isn't began. I noticed that whenever I had been with traditional cultures, this separation was much smaller, or didn't exist at all. Much of the glamour that I had attributed to healers and indigenous cultures, which still have their traditional spirituality intact, was a big projection on my part. After all, these cultures still experience issues and are not utopia. It is important to remember that we visit as tourists and we often see the 'good' bits, but after spending more time with them we begin to see all aspects of their lives, which are just as varied as ours and, in my opinion, much harder. But without having these experiences it is easy to just experience the ecstasy of ceremony and feel that traditional cultures live in constant spiritual rapture. Then it's logical to believe that if we mimic their spirituality, we too may be able to live in endless rapture and all of our issues will fade away. Although an authentic spiritual path *will* undoubtedly help with our issues and our obstacles, it won't simply remove them altogether. The real benefit of spirituality is that it assists us in growing strong enough to deal with our issues so they do not stop us living a happy, peaceful and joyful life. I started to see that the apparent split between the spiritual and the mundane in our culture was just an illusion, and that it was this illusion that was fuelling the Western desire to mimic other cultures and take their exact practices and transplant them into our culture at home. I also saw that this came with huge amounts of sorrow, as it was like fitting a square peg into a round hole, and our culture was different in too many ways for this to work.

This can feel a little deflating. At the time I had this realisation I held my hands up to the sky wondering what to do. So I encourage a more positive reflection. Let us remember what a ritual is. The official definition from the *Cambridge Dictionary* is:

> *an activity or a set of actions that are always*
> *done in the same way or at the same time.*

It really is that simple.

A ritual does not always have to be something very serious and very powerful that only happens in secret forest glades and rocky mountain steppes. A ritual can be the way that we make our morning coffee, or the way we wash our body. It can be how we chop our food, with love, before making dinner for those dear to us. It could be the dog walk we take each morning with our furry best friend.

Of course, these things aren't shamanic – but that doesn't mean that they don't matter.

The more that we can bring ritual into our lives, the better. This is how we can start to transform and breathe life into our culture and rediscover its vibrancy once more. Adding a spiritual quality to our life is about this. It is about being as present as we can be with all of life, not just partaking in exotic ritual and cosplaying traditional cultures. We have no sacred songs left in our land because we see nothing as sacred anymore, so we do not sing to it. Perhaps we can change this.

These cultures practise ritual in exotic places because they *exist* in these places. There is a great teaching in this. They do not travel halfway across the world to find peace, but instead bring peace into their daily life. Their spirituality exists in the places that they live day-to-day, and, inspired by this, we must do the same.

While I often dream of a community sweat ritual in every borough, agreed upon and well-kept laws around the sacred protection of our waters and lands, and community honourings of the local spirits for good luck – I know that isn't realistic for now and it will be a result of many small steps. We must start from the ground up, each taking personal responsibility to wield shamanic and animist teachings in a way that transforms our culture authentically, instead of seeking to bulldoze it and start all over again. We do this by beginning to cultivate an awareness of the importance of reducing the gap between the sacred and the everyday. If we can do this, *then* we can start to build on top of these foundations and cultivate a truly honest spirituality in the West, whose spirituality is effective for us because it is relevant and local.

RITUAL 3

Family-Honouring Ritual

In the West we have lost many of our ancestral honouring ceremonies. Traditional cultures worldwide still partake in individual and communal rituals that honour their ancestors and remember them – giving them praise and honouring so that they can keep their bloodline connection strong.

Ancestral worship is an interesting concept, and although realistically we can only track our ancestral lines back up to ten generations, we are all energy and share the same vibrating atoms that make up existence. We are also ancestors of the animals, plants, earth and the cosmos. We are all family, and, as spoken about in this book, much of the shamanic and animist worldview is based upon this belief of interconnectedness.

A simple ritual to partake in is a family honouring ritual, which can be done individually or collectively, where we repeat our ancestors' story and praise their lives.

- Choose a family member who has passed away and take some time to research their life. You could do this by asking family or using a family tree service online.
- Write them an ode – a ceremonial lyric poem.
- This should include their story, their trials and tribulations, the difficulties and triumphs that they undertook.
- Make sure to praise and thank your ancestor for their life, which has given you your own existence.
- Use 'flowered language' – flamboyant words and rich symbolic, metaphorical language.

- Light a fire, or place a candle on your altar, and honour their memory.
- As you recite the story, sprinkle some of their favourite things into the fire (chocolate, tobacco, etc.). If you have a candle, light it. You do not have to do this, but you can put some fresh fruit and water on your altar.
- This is not a ritual for calling ancestors, but *honouring* and remembering them.

Write down your experiences in your shamanic journal so that you can document how this makes you feel. This can include any dreams or feelings that you experienced as you were speaking your ancestor's story out loud.

CHAPTER 4

Bringing Things Back Down to Earth

I was in my early twenties when I discovered spirituality and, as we have already spoken about, I didn't start with authentic and grounded practices like shamanism. It took me a few years of exploration, but eventually, after a couple years of attending small workshops and reading lots of books, I was lucky enough to begin training as a shamanic practitioner with a well-known teacher in the UK. I would like to say that this is where all my issues stopped and my life became smooth sailing – but that was not the case. Life is never linear, and the healing journey is more like a spiral – sometimes you feel as though you are back to square one.

This chapter is about the need to constantly check in with ourselves on the spiritual path. That although we may be doing all the 'right' things, they may not have the desired outcome. We will talk about the subtleties of healing and spiritual practice, and the huge importance of community, friendship, tribe and subcultures.

* * *

I went downstairs, crept over comatose outstretched legs and grabbed a bin liner, disposing of ashy cans and plates still covered in the remnants of various powders. It was Sunday morning, and the thud of the turntables, debaucherous laughter and general chaos had only ceased an hour or two before. The slightly broken speakers still fuzzed with white noise, and the sound of Lower Clapton Road trickled in through the partly open window, accompanied by sunshine.

I was tired of living in a flat that ended up filled with random people every weekend, so I had just stayed in my room all night, blood boiling, staring at the ceiling. Anyway, I had already told my mates that I was training to be a shamanic healer, so why they couldn't simply wrap their heads around the fact that there was more to life than going out and listening to the same songs, played by the same DJs, with the same people, on the same drugs, was beyond me.

I felt that they were *wasting their lives.*

This could easily be a journal entry from my early twenties. Even though I had been doing exactly the same thing as my flatmates six months earlier, I couldn't handle the fact that they still wanted to do it when I had come to the conclusion that it wasn't serving me. I had spent the last six months proclaiming to anyone who would listen that my identity as a party animal was dead, and that for the near future I was going to be 'a healer' instead.

I was prone to obsession and I had found my new one. The first step of this transformation was changing my clothes, and I swapped my Air Max for Vibrams (barefoot shoes that have individual toe compartments), and my sportswear made way for loose cardigans and floaty trousers. After the costume was sorted, it was time for the soundtrack, and, to my grave annoyance to this day, I deleted hours upon hours of underground music, replacing it with the soothing sounds of the bansuri and other assorted tribal melodies instead. After this came the difficult part, which was finding a way to put together my newfound identity with my life. I even gave up one of my prized possessions, my Tottenham Hotspur season ticket. Swiftly and surely, I cut ties with anything that connected me to my past in search of new beginnings.

Over the next few months, as I continued my training and isolated myself further, I started to experience a mental breakdown as I lost touch with reality and my 'normal world'. My mental health fell apart, stripping me of my confidence as I descended into paranoia and confusion. I started to feel weak and fragile. In search of some form of respite I just delved further into my spiritual practice – blaming those around me for my own discomfort.

It seems so simple now, as I look back, that isolating myself, engaging in hardcore shamanic training, plying my mind with hallucinogens and turning my back on everything that I knew, almost overnight, would have a detrimental effect on my mental health. But at the time I genuinely felt that it was something that I needed to do. I also didn't have any other guidance, or somebody that I could talk to who had been in the position that I was in. Nowadays, I occasionally get messages from people who are in the same spot that I was, confused that they still suffer immensely even though they are doing vast amounts of spiritual work and have put huge amounts of effort into leaving their old lives behind. This can be very frustrating for them because they are doing everything that they 'should' be doing according to the spiritual path, but still encounter obstacles.

They are often relieved to hear my answer: 'Slow down and stop trying to be so spiritual for a while.'

We Westerners tend to have a habit with spiritual practice of doing things too fast and too soon. The spiritual path can be incredibly exciting and alluring – it was for me. Due to the way that much of Western spiritual culture is set up – for profit – if we can pay, we can have access to extremely advanced techniques and practices and nobody to tell us that we aren't ready for them. This is different to traditional cultures, where a lineage holder (an elder who safeguards the lineage and its practices) will only permit you to practise something if you have proven yourself capable by mastering the practices that come before. This level of verification not only protects the lineage from being diluted by those who don't practise properly, but it also safeguards the budding practitioner from gaining access to power that they are not ready for, and protects their sense of self and identity enough so that they can remain stable while evolving at the right pace for them. I paid the price for diving into the deep end too fast, and psychologically it was very difficult for me.

If we separate from what we know too fast we may start to experience a sense of disorientation that can be very detrimental to our mental health. It's in our DNA to belong, and we are hardwired for connection – not just to feel happy, but to prevent our psyches from going into survival mode. Feeling a sense of belonging and being connected to a group is extremely important for our wellbeing. Included in this recipe are our social traditions, the memories we have with others, a sense of togetherness through hardship and struggle, and our personal social identity within a group. Our lives are meaningful, in a large way, because of these things – even if they are not necessarily *always* net positive for you. A well-timed beer with close friends can be more healing than a badly held ayahuasca retreat. It is all in the details and the nuances of life, and doing spiritual things because of the labels that accompany them may be more detrimental than beneficial. In my own situation, although on paper I was becoming more 'spiritual', my patience and compassion for others went straight out the window. Although my crown chakra may have opened a little bit, my heart closed a lot. I sacrificed my humanity for my spirituality – and this is all too easy a trap to fall into.

Compassion is the most important part of any spiritual practice, and if we start to lose it we are going in the wrong direction. Compassion is so important to our lives that our evolution from asocial reptiles to social mammals depended on it, and the transformative capacity to work together and assist each other that it brings propelled us into consciousness. Darwin's theory of survival of the fittest is often assumed to mean that the 'fittest' are the physically strongest. In reality the animals with the highest chance of survival are those that are the most emotionally intelligent and interact and co-operate with each other. Evolutionary biologist Theodosius Dobzhansky interprets Darwin's theory as: 'The fittest may also be the gentlest, because survival often requires mutual help and co-operation.'

Our huge capacity for compassion is why humans have succeeded everywhere on earth. Experiencing a lack of compassion in ourselves, and from others, has been increasingly proven to be detrimental to physical and mental health. A meta-analytic review found that isolation and a lack of positive social relationships increase the over-all risk of death in the same way as well-established risk factors, such as smoking and obesity, and a recent MIT study found that we crave social engagement in the same region of our brains that we crave food when we are fasting – pointing towards this being a basic human need. Chronic social isolation and a lack of compassion and belonging is associated with lower mental and physical health. Another study at the University of Michigan found that lacking a sense of belonging is a precursor to depression. Our mental health can also be affected detrimentally when we are unable to authentically express ourselves to those within our community. A meta-analysis of independent studies of authenticity and its relationship to wellbeing found that those who believed that they were able to live authentically also felt they had more meaningful lives, which in turn led to more happiness, peace and contentment.

If you add all of these outcomes to the already difficult process of healing, we start to paint a picture of a very difficult situation. Healing our traumas, even within a community setting, can be incredibly challenging and disorientating. But doing so *alone* is even more difficult, and, with no support network to offer safe and secure spaces in which to rest and recuperate, many people can completely fall apart as they get utterly overwhelmed – which is what happened to me. If I could go back in time,

I would advise myself to go much slower than I did. Although it may feel urgent, in reality there is absolutely no rush to let go of trauma and evolve on the spiritual path. Letting go of parts of ourself, and of parts of our life that represent them, is often necessary at some point within our journey, but we can only let go properly if we are ready to do so. It cannot be forced, and if we do this when we are not ready it can be overwhelming. The best thing that we can do is to hold on to as much stability as possible while we lean into our practices, trusting that they will enable us to heal at the pace that we are meant to. Start with a simple practice – a ritual from this book, or an authentic beginner's meditation from another practice and teacher – and master it. Spiritual practice can only flourish as far as the foundations that support it – so it is really important to take your time, especially in the early years.

If possible, you do not have to do this alone either. As we can see, community is essential! Ironically, even though I was on my own shamanic path, by leaving my communities I was making it impossible to move forward, as I had no stability, compassion or joy around me. I was forgetting an essential part of earth-centric practice, which is that all animist and shamanic cultures are focussed around community. This helps those within them to (amongst other things) share the burden of healing. A person who is going through a healing crisis is brought back into the culture, cared for and nurtured. Although our culture is becoming much wiser and more understanding when it comes to mental health issues, there can still be an unfair stigma around those who suffer with them, and this stigma can make them even harder to deal with. I also often speak to people who feel confined by clinical labels and diagnoses, which can feel like immovable labels. The truth, though, is that our mental health waxes and wanes throughout life depending on many factors, and feeling accepted and honoured despite how we may feel inside can go a long way to restabilising ourselves after becoming unbalanced. Care, love, respect and compassionate presence can soothe a person deeply.

But with all that said, understanding our tribe, our family and our communities can be a difficult task. Ultimately, it is a combination of all three that provides us with all of the elements we need to flourish as human beings – so let's explore them in more detail.

TRIBE, FAMILY AND COMMUNITY

Our tribe is something that we are born into, a non-negotiable starting point in the world. Sometimes people can reject their tribe, for their own reasons – some of which may be valid. Nonetheless, our origins play a part in who we are and who we will become. My tribe is England, which is a source of great pride but also some mixed emotion for me. Alongside and emerging from tribe comes our family – which is another non-negotiable starting point in the world, where we inherit much of who we are. It is then into community where many of us are drawn in order to catapult ourselves from the clutches of these sturdy but sometimes confining traditions and seek our own individuality.

For many of us in the West, our tribe and our family can seem limiting and regressive. We may feel as though they do not support the flourishing of our individuality. Instead, the views and traditions of our tribe and family often seem more concerned with maintaining the status quo – or the collective group consciousness. For many of us, we look around the world and it feels as though the traditions of the West have become stale and are in need of renewal. But still they hold a lot of power – the energy from tribe and family can be so strong that it can overwhelm and completely contain an individual, preventing them from ever exploring and connecting with their own inherent sense of self. On a macro scale we can see examples of this in long-standing feuds between countries and cultures that continue into future generations, who have no real reason to feel the same animosity towards each other. On a micro scale we may see this in our own families as we minimise our own goals and dreams in order to receive acceptance and respect from our parents. In both examples the individual consciousness of a person has been swallowed by the larger tribal or familial consciousness. This is not all bad though. The seemingly everlasting consciousness of the tribe provides safety. There is safety in numbers, after all, and tradition provides this sense of security – even if that tradition feels outdated. It is a wonderful feeling to be accepted by our parents, and there is nothing wrong with seeking their approval. Because tribe consciousness and family consciousness originally emerge from survival (as we explored earlier in the chapter), the psychological stakes of breaking free from both tribal and familial consciousness are very high, and huge courage and bravery must be cultivated to do so. So we are left in a slightly tricky position. But despite this, we must at some point individuate if we are to become our own person and connect to something deeper within ourselves. It is here that communities come in. A well-intentioned community provides a new space in which to explore the flourishing and emerging consciousness of our personal soul. Community allows for a freedom of expression outside of the traditional boundaries of tribe and family, and affords us the opportunity to disidentify from its sometimes stifling rigidity. Community is *emergent*, and is where many people 'find themselves' and develop their identity. Community allows for a deepening of the relationship to self amongst others who are doing the same, which is a beautiful and powerful thing. I found it myself within the rave scene and then eventually in the shamanic community. I needed to leave behind the patterns and behaviours of my tribe and family in order to embark on my personal journey to find out who I was and forge my own unique identity. But what I found here is that – although a healing journey may take us from tribe to family and then to community – it is not a linear progression that ends with community as a finishing line. Instead, once individual consciousness has been developed within emergent communities, a reclamation of tribe and family must happen so that the individual gifts that have been uncovered within community can be shared back and can renew them in turn. An analogy can be made with a fruit tree. The tribe is the tree, and the family are the branches. Community then acts as the fruit that emerges and allows for the reproduction of the tree, bringing new life and renewal. Without this emergence of fruit the tree itself soon becomes rigid and lifeless. This cycle allows us to infuse the gift of our own individuation back into world for the greater good.

In the same way that remaining in tribal or familial consciousness risks never fully emerging as an individual, if we do not make the journey back to reclaim our tribe and family it can create self-serving parts of society that turn their backs on their roots and give nothing back to the greater good. This either isolates them, or forms a divide of an 'us against them' mentality. A community that is severed from tribe and family is unable to feed back its life-giving qualities to the culture as a whole, and as a result starts to detach itself from reality. Within the fruit tree analogy – the fruit rots and never meets the earth again to carry on the cycle of life. This is how community becomes cult, and with no roots in tribe and family to bring it back down to earth, a reversal of the consciousness expansion that made the community so great in the first place starts to happen, and the community inevitably starts to eat itself from the inside.

If we think of some successful movements in the West, we can see this cycle at play and how it has been able to feed back the emergent and nourishing energy to tribe and family to renew culture as a whole. The underground music scene that flourished in Britain in the 1980s and 1990s altered the perception of the working class and marginalised peoples for the whole country. It provided a sound that reverberated around the world and gave young people a renewed sense of purpose that cut through Margaret Thatcher's archaic politics. While the tribe, and the families, originally felt threatened and concerned about what thousands of young people were doing every weekend in warehouses and fields, eventually the mainstream came to accept the movement and it has now filtered through to all parts of our society. In my generation, drum and bass, jungle, UK garage and dubstep are sounds that began as underground movements but have made a huge impact on our culture, doing the same as acid house and punk did in the previous generations. Music brings people together and unites all races, creeds and religions under its banner. The tolerance and joy this creates then spreads and gives members of society, who previously felt disempowered, new purpose and opportunities, thus changing the outlook of the tribes and families throughout the UK.

Football is also a huge part of my life, and learning this cycle motivated me to reclaim my beloved Tottenham Hotspur season ticket. There is much tribal and spiritual significance in football. Teams are often handed down to us from our ancestors who have local links to them. There is shared ancestral experience within it, as each week we get together to watch our beloved team. For me, every two weeks I, like my ancestors, partake in a ritual with members of my Tottenham tribe – meeting at the station, going to the pub, and then congregating in the stadium (in a circle) to sing songs and celebrate our team. There is even a good deal of prayer that goes on (especially if you support Tottenham Hotspur). There is a wonderful sense of belonging in football that allows each person to settle into the tribal holding and let go of their personal identity. Nobody cares about what job you do, or your political views. For those few hours, all that matters is Tottenham Hotspur and the identity that we share by being there. We shout obscenities, laugh hysterically, cry like babies, and jump on and kiss each other ecstatically when a goal goes in. The emotion behind all of these actions is real, but the acts that are being celebrated are ritualised in a way that *gives* them permission to be acted out. I would never act like this outside of the ritual container of 'the matchday experience'. Football was the first place that I could be emotional and vulnerable with other men. Ritualised events that bring us together like this, allowing us to express and process emotion, are of huge value to our society. But within this beauty, we see the tribal elements of regression that still exist. The fierce and strong tribal consciousness still regularly overtakes the individual – within these tribal group dynamics people can find themselves acting in ways that they never would outside football, but this time in a negative sense. Collective energy and power build and build until they explode out and the old collective tribal rivalries 'possess' people – they are taken over by emotion that often leads to violence. In group settings of shared intention like this, the shadow side of people often finds its way to the surface as they feel connected to a larger sense of power and indestructability. Discriminatory behaviours such as racism and sexism, which usually exist under the surface, bubble their way to the top and it becomes a horrible thing. This is where emergent community needs to keep coming into football to change it. For when community starts to flourish within football it can have hugely positive ramifications for tribe. Clubs taking action and bringing awareness to racism, the rise of the women's league and LGTBQ movements have already begun to feed new views back into the tribal consciousness of football, allowing for the emergence of new beliefs and for old patterns to be renewed, which starts to alter the perception of those connected to the tribe, creating change.

Shamanic and animist cultures hold their traditions and 'tribe' in very high regard. This is evident when you visit one of these cultures. Their tribe and their traditions are a source of great pride and identity for them, and this in turn means that these cultures, in my experience, are less individualistic than the West. But what is different within their tribal pride is the regular use of ritual in order to renew themselves to stay connected to the life-giving energies of the earth that sustain them. The in-built rituals of shamanic cultures support the expansion of individual consciousness and then feed this renewal back into the greater good. This is the difference between these traditions and the West. Whereas in our culture tribe and family are often disconnected from community, in traditional cultures they are entwined. Our culture at present does not support renewal from within the tribe, so in order to develop our individual consciousness we must often each seek out countercultural movements to find ourselves. This makes it a harder process for us, as we must take it upon ourselves to act as tricksters and go against what we know in order to find healing. In traditional cultures the inherent values of that culture already support heart-opened change and the development of deeper levels of consciousness, which they understand help all parts of that culture. Looking at it this way, it is clear to me that our sub-culture communities have huge potential for us. When our youth is drawn to them, their rebellion can actually be a very important form of growth, and we should encourage their behaviour and not shame it, for in the undertones of their behaviour there is so much to learn from. This will help to reconnect our youth with the elders of our culture, which starts to renew it in a sacred way, greatly helping the wisdom gained from community to filter back into the wider consciousness of tribe and family.

RITUAL 4

Water-Honouring Ritual

I was going through a difficult time once, and I asked a Colombian medicine man how I could start to work through my emotions. He told me that the way he learnt was to make time to pray to the water. He said that as we are roughly 60 per cent water, it is the water that rules our emotions and we can petition the spirit of water for assistance.

This is the ritual that I did, and over time it really helped me to cultivate a deeper relationship with water as a sacred element, and in turn my emotions, which ebb and flow just as water does.

- Set an alarm for 4 am. This is an auspicious time between night and day – a liminal space that is powerful for prayer and spiritual practice.
- Come to your altar and clean the space with sacred smoke, as instructed in the previous rituals.
- Fill a cup with water. Natural spring water is best, but any water will do.
- Sit in silence with the cup in your hands.
- Steady your breath and do your best to focus your awareness on the water.
- As you focus on the water, begin to pray out loud to the sacred waters of the world, offering them complimentary words and thanking the entire element of water from a deep place of gratitude, for water is life, and without it we cannot live.
- As you pray, slowly and mindfully imagine cool and sacred water washing over you from your head to your toes

and cleansing you of difficult emotions, not just cleansing you outside, but inside too, running through and cleansing your entire being.

- Let this process unfold as slowly as it needs to.
- Place the water out in nature with gratitude.

Write down your experiences in your shamanic journal so that you can document how this makes you feel. This can include any dreams, or feelings that you experienced as you were performing this ritual.

CHAPTER 5

Story Time

Humans are woven together by story. Stories are how we relate to one another. They assist us in orienting ourselves in the world and inform us of how we remember the past and how we imagine the future. I would go so far as to say that without stories, nothing in this world exists for us. I have been incredibly fortunate to experience the work of several wonderful teachers and the one thing that they all had in common was that they all understood the huge value and importance of stories.

Your personal story, your ancestral story, your cultural story, the earth's story and countless other stories are constantly rubbing up against, pulling, pushing, absorbing and rejecting each other in a beautiful and unimaginably intricate dance. In the centre of that dance, each of us exists. When it comes to healing, some of these stories – our family and personal stories – may trap us. Forcing us to believe that we are not capable of healing, and that to exist outside of these stories means to not exist at all. But some of these stories – the earth's story or our cultural story – may empower us – giving us the strength to connect to larger powers than us, and imbuing us with the confidence to step out of our comfort zone and into new ways of being.

Art, mythology and legend are important parts of all cultures. The difference between our brain and that of the neanderthal is our enhanced ability to communicate with symbolic representation, which allows us to plan and scheme, but has also led to story, music and art. In a big way this is what made us the humans that we are today – the passing down, and preservation, of the stories of each culture's cosmological beginnings are of vital importance to the survival of that tradition. Without these there is no start point. No 'staff in the ground' that the threads of that culture can be woven around to clothe their identity. Without knowing where and what you come from, it is impossible to know what you are.

It is hard to come to terms with the true importance of storytelling as a Westerner. Within it there is a deepness and a richness that is hard to comprehend. This is perhaps a little ironic, as we are the ones who have witnessed the era of billion-dollar blockbuster movies and iconic movie stars, some of which have been elevated to an almost celestial status. But we rarely let these stories unfold within us, and in general we watch stories, or read them, to *escape* from life, rather than to dive in and swim *amongst* it.

We see mythologies as playful stories about things that

never *really* happened. Folktales are for children and hold little meaning for grown-ups, and local legends are just that – echoes of faint murmurings from a time gone by, not bearing much significance for a city dweller sitting on the train with their flat white.

But this is a tragedy, and we shall see that by forgetting what stories mean for us, in their most sacred sense, we are cut off from vital energy that can greatly assist with our personal and collective healing. We have already spoken of the benefits of belonging and identity when it comes to our psychological health. This chapter lets us delve into more detail into the purpose and meaning that our cultural and family surroundings bring us. We look into the importance of cultural and family stories, and how this can benefit us on our healing journey. As always, we will also look at traditional animist and shamanic cultures, to take inspiration for how we can start to live our lives more authentically.

LOCAL CULTURAL STORY

A connection to our local cultural story provides us with a firm sense of identity and pride that can help to prop us up in times of struggle. At the start of the pandemic I moved to a small town in the Midlands called Dudley, where my wife is from. Living there for two years, it was easy to sense a harking back to older times when the city was a thriving jewel of the Black Country, with a bustling coal mine at the centre of it. Her ancestors, like many others in the city, were miners. While mining was an incredibly difficult life and came with many dangers, including early death through an illness called pneumoconiosis, it gave the city real pride and sense of meaning. From speaking to people, it seemed as though the miners, and their family members, felt that through their work they provided a crucial service to the industries of the country. There was also a shared connection with their ancestors, as many of them had followed in the footsteps of their fathers and grandfathers. When I spoke to anybody above the age of sixty, although they spoke with a burning passion of their pride that they were from Dudley, they were also in agreement that the city had begun to fall from its former glory when the mines had closed in 1968. It was almost like a spell had been cast, and the cultural sense of disempowerment at the loss of a strong sense of meaning was palpable. There wasn't just a sense that they lost their jobs and income – which was bad enough – but they also lost their purpose. The town never recovered, as that purpose was never replaced with anything as meaningful as mining. Slowly they lost a lot of their traditions, such as local working dialect and songs about the area, and many young people forgot their roots. With that they lost their ties to the past and the shared ancestral experience. Walking through Baggeridge Country Park, where the last mine shaft was closed on 2 March

1968, I often thought about the miners toiling all day in the mines. I thought about the backbreaking work and them getting home after a long day underground, covered in mud and coal, aching and sore but perhaps propped up by knowing that they were part of an enchanting story that connected them with their fathers and their grandfathers – a story that brought enough meaning to supplement their difficult struggle with a fierce sense of belonging.

Something happens when you add purpose and meaning to struggle and pain. Suddenly a negative experience can become transformative instead of disempowering. In this example, on a local cultural level this could be undertaking backbreaking work in the mines but knowing that you provide an essential service for your community, and feeling the pride that they feel for you. But on a more personal and modern level, I often see the ramifications of feeling that pain and struggle has no purpose. To bring this back to healing and shamanism, regularly in my one-to-one practice people turn up with an array of issues and confusion around their symptomatology. They do not understand why they suffer so much, and have come to the conclusion that it must be because they are inherently bad people, or that they are cursed. With a little digging and a perspective shift, they can find some kind of meaning in their pain and realise that their suffering has a deeper wisdom that symbolises something beautiful unfurling on a more mysterious level. This could be as simple as realising that the reason that they are so anxious is because there is a part of them that never received the love and care that they needed as an infant. This is common, as so often we develop behaviours and beliefs in our early years in order to shield us from the devastating effects of emotional or physical neglect. The start of a healing journey may be the process of a person learning their personal and familial story so that they are able to shift it in a way that makes it empowering rather than disempowering. By understanding the roots of their story and the behaviours, needs and wants of the parts of themselves still locked within that story, suddenly, without actually doing any 'healing' work, their relationship to their anxiety has shifted from one of aversion, to welcoming these wounded aspects of themselves with open arms. The truth that these uncomfortable thoughts and emotions originally arose as great protectors of their fragility becomes illuminated, and each wave of anxiety provides them with an opportunity to soothe their inner infant with compassion and love. It is still a painful process, but all of a sudden their pain has meaning and their confusion around it is lifted. This causes a shift in their story about themselves and now healing can begin. There is still struggle, but it has shifted from the struggle of pushing parts of themselves away, to bringing them closer.

* * *

Part of why indigenous spirituality is so powerful for Westerners is because these cultures have many of their local cultural stories intact. When you experience a traditional ceremony, it is a very moving and meaningful experience, not only because of the magic that is created through working with the spirits, but also because there is a timelessness to the ritual that makes it feel incredibly special and precious. For a Westerner this can feel as though you have been transported back to the beginning of human history. From a healing perspective this is massive, as it offers the opportunity to rewrite your personal story from the ground up. This is transformational in itself, and just being part of a community ritual that has unblemished authenticity soothes the soul, and sometimes no other deep work is needed. There is also a great power that gains momentum within a tradition. Over time the power is compacted and becomes something incredibly strong. This power forms a protective energy around the community, which helps to hold the fabric of that community together. For a Westerner this almost seems like a dream, but one that we respond to very deeply because this kind of community living and ritual is in our DNA. In the West we all come from shamanic, animist or pagan societies, but even in more recent times – when we would have subscribed to monotheistic religions – community rituals and local stories, myths and legends assisted our communities with the struggles of life by providing a sense of meaning and connection. I have also observed certain everyday symbols and objects that are used within these traditional rituals. It feels as though these become empowered through the ritual – whether that is the hearth fire in Mongolia, the deer or corn in Mexico, or the baobab tree in Senegal. These sacred symbols play a huge part in both the sacred and everyday life of the culture, which helps those within that culture to bridge the gap between the sacred and the mundane, and stay connected to the life-giving energies of the spirit world. It also connects their personal lives to the deeper meaning that exists in their culture. In an animist sense these symbols and objects are alive with their own spirits who, if a community is in right relation with them, offer protection and balance. The sense of belonging and pride that this brings a person should not be underestimated.

In comparison, and going back to our current spiritual culture, the New Age employs many symbols, but very few of them are symbols or objects that we also find in our everyday lives. Instead they are usually picked from other cultures and transplanted into Western culture, where the same power that belongs to these symbols is not present – such as the *om* and the yin-yang, or exotic feathers and plants that do not exist here. There is nothing inherently wrong with this, but it is important to note that these will not have the same power here as they do in their original environment. There are also repurposed symbols from long-gone Celtic and Norse animistic traditions, such as the spiral triskele and runes, which lack the same power that they would have had in the past. The use of these symbols often means that, when we enter the spiritual space of the New Age, it is difficult to integrate the power of ritual into our daily lives because these symbols simply don't exist there. This can encourage the viewpoint that in order to stay connected to the numinous we must somehow leave behind the ordinary and change our identities, which does not need to be the case.

Instead, to me it makes sense to find something that exists both within the spiritual ritual and our everyday, just like traditional cultures do so well. This way we can stay connected like they do, instead of partaking in extra-curricular spiritual activities that are hard to integrate. A good way to do this is to find something that you have in your home that connects you with your ancestors – something you both would have had. A fireplace is a wonderful place to do this. The hearth fire has been with humans since the beginning, and our ancestors would have honoured it as sacred. If you have a fireplace, I invite you to make this a sacred place. Do not put rubbish in the fire or anything dirty, keep it lit often and feed it with some of the food that you make. Treat it like a member of your family and honour the warmth and protection that it gives you and gave your ancestors. If you do not have a fireplace, you could instead perform an act that your ancestors would have done – such as baking bread. Do this with love and presence, honouring the process. Share it amongst your family and friends, gifting warm and nourishing food to others who are in need. It is these small and precious things that we must bring awareness to if we are to evolve spiritually as a culture.

Another thing that brings these indigenous cultures power is that their spirituality is incredibly local. We have already spoken about how much of traditional earth-centric spirituality is formed around landmarks local to the culture that practises it. The centre point of their entire cosmology may be a local mountain, a tree, a lake or another local landmark that the village or community life is based around. As we now know, within the animist worldview these landmarks are enlivened and owned by the spirits that inhabit them. This enables these cultures to live and breathe their spirituality, which is yet another way that allows them to stay connected to themselves and their ancestors. This is also why we must start to look to our own landscape at some point, and why cultural appropriation is such an issue – not only because of the obvious degradation and insult to traditional cultures. Picking up and transplanting a culture from a far-off land into our modern lives, but not also bringing the landscape, which is inhabited by the local spirits that give it the power in the first place, renders it much less effective in terms of healing. Without a real connection to the spirits and landscape of the culture that you are mimicking, all that can be hoped for is a sort of cosplay that both dilutes the original culture and brings bad karma for those that partake. This does not mean that you shouldn't explore traditions from other cultures, but if you do wish to pursue that path then I would highly recommend finding an authentic teacher belonging to an authentic lineage, who will be able to guide you on your path and connect you to that particular culture.

FAMILY STORY

We spoke of the rigidity of the family story in the last chapter. But let's delve into that more, and why they can be so difficult to step away from when we need to heal. Our inherited family story is strong and can easily define who we are if we are not able to break out of the binding patterns that accompany it. Overall, I was very lucky with my family, and there is a lot of love shared between us all. However, there is a theme of dysfunction in romantic relationships that runs at least three generations into the past, where divorce and infidelity are very present. I'm not alone in experiencing this – in the UK and Wales over the last fifty years one-third of marriages have ended in divorce, and one in five people report that they have been unfaithful when in a committed relationship. On a personal (and anecdotal!) level I would say at least three-quarters of my close friends also grew up experiencing the divorce of their caregivers. It is fair to say it is a big issue in the West, and my own experiences with it have shaped my life in a huge way. Due to my experience growing up I inherited my own dysfunctions around partnerships and found it very difficult to form healthy romantic relationships. I often became completely dependent on my partners for making me feel safe, as I couldn't really deal with the emotions that sprung up around love. This developed into OCD and manifested in me compulsively bombarding my partners with questions about their past. I knew this was hugely irritating for my partners and I would try to make it up to them by desperately trying to prove my worth in other areas where I acted like the 'perfect' partner – buying gifts, taking them to nice places, and sacrificing my own needs for theirs. The reason for these compulsive questions all stemmed back to needing to feel safe and weigh up my chances of them being unfaithful to me. Each time I tried to resist asking questions, I would become so anxious that I would have a panic attack. It was as if there was some-thing in me driving this behaviour, even though I didn't want to do it, and knew it was destructive and dysfunc-tional, I felt powerless against it.

This is an example of a familial story loop that we can often find ourselves in. An original wounding derived from our family line drives a deep fear – in my case a fear of abandonment. As a way to mitigate this deep fear we develop compulsions – in my case a compulsion to find out everything I could about my partner's past through interrogation. But instead of actually helping, these compulsions just keep us 'locked into' the fear as the emotional charge behind them never gets released or soothed. Ultimately I realised that no matter the answers I would receive from my partners, I would never feel safe until I healed the wound that I had inherited from my parents. Unsurprisingly, until I took responsibility for my own wounding, my partners would inevitably get so sick of me asking questions that they would either leave me or be unfaithful – which only provided more 'proof' for this deep fear to stay relevant – continuing the loop. I knew I had to make a change if I had any chance of enjoying love, but nothing I had tried had really helped. I had received psychotherapy, energy healing and a myriad of other techniques, and had worked on it for years at this point, but nothing had really done much to shift this deep fear of losing my partners. Eventually, enough was enough, and with no other option I prayed to my spirits for assistance.

They told me that the issues had begun with my great-grandmother. I had always been very close to her when she was alive, but she'd passed away when I was eight or nine. It was the first time that I had experienced death and I remember it deeply affecting me. In my shamanic training, she often showed up during ceremonies and she was a real anchor point for me, so my spirits informing me that our family issues began with her surprised me, as she had always seemed the most normal! It suddenly dawned on me that I had never met her husband, or realised that she'd even had one. It was as if he had either not existed at all or had been forgotten by the entire family. I asked my grand-mother about it and she said that they had never spoken about him much. He had confessed to my great-grandmother that he had another family – a wife and children – and that he was choosing them over her and the children that they had had together. This obviously left her incredibly hurt and traumatised. In the 1940s especially, this was a huge source of shame and she never remarried. This massive distrust around relationships with others was then fed down to her children, who inherited these beliefs around love as they had also been left and abandoned by their father for another family. This fed into their own relationship dynamics and the cycle continued into my mother, and then into me. My spirits told me that a ritual was needed and that I was to take two candles (one for my great-grandmother and one for my great-grandfather), take them out to nature with specific offerings of flowers, coins, nuts and a ribbon for each candle, plant them at the base of a specific tree, and pray to both of their spirits to come back together and sort out their differences for the benefit of the family. I then had to be strong and resist any habitual compulsions that arose from this trauma, trusting that the healing had occurred, and commit to discontinuing my destructive behaviour. In short – no more questions. This was my part of the bargain, which is so often the case with shamanic or animistic healing.

In shamanic belief unresolved trauma like this is often handed down the family lines until it is healed. While it is very difficult to go back and heal the ancestors who have passed, we can create conditions for them to forgive the pain, and this can reduce the burden on those in the line who are still living with the effects of it. While this can seem like a woo-woo idea – we don't have to look far to see that many families continue the traumatic traditions and behaviours of their forebears – addictions and abuse often run in families. The cycle is perpetuated, as a person often treats others how they are treated themselves, and people become trapped in the family loop.

Shortly after finding this information out from both my spirits and my grandmother I went and performed the ceremony. There was no great moment of healing or power, it was all very matter-of-fact and practical. I didn't tell anybody in my family that I was doing it either, but a week later I received a call from my grandmother. She explained that since she'd spoken to me about my great-grandmother she had started to feel a huge weight move from her chest. She said that the tension she had experienced related to this situation all throughout her life had started to lift, and she wasn't sure why. A couple of weeks later my mother spoke to me and said that she had started to finally accept and come to terms with the guilt of divorcing my father, and although she always knew it was the right decision, she had started to make peace with the fallout of her actions. A month later my father, who was from a completely different bloodline but had been affected all the same as my mother had divorced him, rang me to tell me that he had finally 'woken up' and realised that the woman he had married after my mother wasn't right for him, and that he was leaving that marriage in order to continue with his life. It was as though he had snapped out of a trance and that his personal power had been returned. A few months later he was in a new relationship with a woman he then married, and he has never seemed happier. For me, after a tricky few weeks navigating the mental patterns left over from years of compulsive thinking, I eventually conquered the habit. The sting of them had greatly diminished shortly after the ceremony and I no longer had panic attacks when I resisted the compulsion to ask questions. This made it so much easier to sit with them and unravel the truth underneath them, that all I really wanted was to feel loved – something that my partner was much more likely to do if I stopped pushing them away with questions! It became much easier for me to settle into relationships.

I finally conquered my issues of mistrust. I'm married now, and I don't think it would have been possible without this shamanic assistance.

This is an example of the power of shamanic ritual and the endless wisdom of the spirits. I hardly had any experience when I performed this self-help ritual and simply followed the instructions from the spirits that I had started to work with during my training. This was a huge step for me as I began to understand the power of the spirit world from lived experience rather than intellectually. My family transformed before my eyes, and – although we are still a little rough around the edges – the past seems to have been put back in its rightful place! It shows that if we create the right conditions in the spirit world we can deeply transform our daily reality. My great-grandmother and great-grandfather never got the chance to meet and settle their differences when they were alive, so it took somebody in the family to create the conditions for that to happen in the afterlife to create the same outcome. I encourage you to think about your family line and how the actions of your forebears have affected it. If you are not familiar with your ancestors, it is a very useful exercise to learn who they were and where you came from. We are extensions of them, and vice versa. Our family stories hold so many clues for us on our healing journey, and sometimes the pain that we carry did not begin with us.

RITUAL 5

Fire-Honouring Ritual

The Western relationship to fire is in need of a shift. Our relentless drive for success, our capitalist and colonial expansions and our corporations that chomp and devour the natural world are driven by an imbalanced relationship to fire. Fire has the capacity for great harm – a ferocious blaze can wipe out almost anything in the natural world. Traditional cultures understand this destructive capability, and to stay in right relations with the fire element is seen as of vital importance, be this in their local environment (with many traditional cultures partaking in controlled burning of forest areas in order to stimulate new growth and life) or psychologically (with the exuberance of youth being tempered by tough initiations in order to cultivate their potentially reckless inner fire into something beneficial).

Fire may destroy if left unchecked and if it is fed with too much fuel. But fire is also the sun – the most important celestial body that we have. Fire is daybreak, which lights the way in the darkest of times, and fire is the heart of the home, which warms us when we need it most. It is said that wherever humans have gone in the world, they have carried two things – language and fire. It is these two ingredients that create tradition, bring hope, and inspire us to live.

There are two ways that one can undertake the following fire ritual.

If you have a fireplace, please use this ritual.

WHAT YOU NEED

- Matches or a lighter
- Kindling
- A bowl of offerings – nuts, oats, chocolate and tobacco (if you use it in a sacred way)
- A rattle (you can fill a glass jar with salt or seeds if you do not have one)

INSTRUCTIONS

- Make sure the area around your fireplace is clean.

- Prepare your kindling and build a structure that will easily light (you can research online if you do not know how to do this). It does not have to be big – it only needs to burn for fifteen to thirty minutes.
- Have your bowl of offerings next to you.
- Light the fire, and when it has caught, begin to rattle.
- While rattling, use the sound to focus your attention on the flames. Watch them as you start to connect to the repetitive sound of the rattle.
- If any sounds or words come to you – express yourself to the fire.
- As you start to feel connected to the fire – take a handful of your offerings and offer them to the flames.
- Say a prayer of gratitude to the fire, as always, praying with symbolic language.
- Thank the fire and pray that you are able to balance your internal fires, so that they may become nourishing and inspiring, instead of destructive.

Write down your experiences in your shamanic journal so that you can document how this makes you feel. This can include any emotions or visions that you experienced as you were performing this ritual.

If you do not have a fireplace, please use this ritual.

WHAT YOU NEED

- A candle big enough to burn for three nights (around thirty hours)
- A jar big enough to hold the whole candle
- Some sand
- Matches or a lighter

INSTRUCTIONS

- Fill the bottom of the jar with 1cm of sand.
- Place the candle in the sand.
- Make sure that the candle is at least level with your upper body, not facing your feet (this can be seen as disrespectful to the fire).

- As you go to sleep, light the candle and place the jar in a safe place.
- As you light the candle, pray to be shown in your dreams how you can balance your relationship with the element of fire.
- When you awaken in the morning, extinguish the flame.

Write your dreams in your shamanic journal so that you remember them.

CHAPTER 6

Magical Thinking – the Great Debate

I found writing this chapter the most difficult in the book. I went back and forth on just how to approach the topic of magical thinking, which is an important one when we are talking about spiritual practice and healing. On one hand, in the West, we need more magical thinking. Opening up to the possibility that there is more to life than meets the eye can open up opportunities to us for amazing healing and growth, and for most of us, the animist worldview that much of this book is based on relies on some form of magical thinking. On the other hand, there *is* an over-emphasis on magical thinking within the spiritual communities of the West, which are prone to projection and conspiracy, as we shall explore. Too much of this can lead to a lack of clarity, confusion and distrust. So we are left with a paradox, where we need to both push and pull. With that in mind, let's explore both sides of the argument and the benefits, and issues, that they bring – hopefully landing somewhere in the middle together.

THE POSITIVES OF MAGICAL THINKING

Magical thinking is most often used as a term to describe the belief that unrelated events are causally connected despite the absence of any plausible causal link, alongside the belief that one's thoughts alone can influence the material world. The issue with this definition is that it depends on the cultural worldview of the person who is deciding whether something is related or not, and then again on the cultural definition of just how it is possible to 'influence' the material world with the mind. Within the modern rationalistic and scientific worldview, for example, a person falling sick would not be seen to be related to them having angered a water spirit – so this would be termed magical thinking and seen as irrational. But to an animist or shamanic culture, these two things would not be seen as unrelated or coincidental, but very much connected, and this would not be considered magical thinking at all, but an ordinary and logical thought process. Much of a shaman's healing ability also comes from the power and great capacity of their well-trained and powerful mind – so it is indeed possible for thoughts to have an impact on the material world. But this is vastly different to the mind of an ordinary person who has not undergone the extensive training that a shaman would have.

In the first chapter of this book we spoke about healing

from a shamanic perspective, and the difference between Western and shamanic forms of medicine. Whereas the Western practitioner will often address the symptom first, and then perhaps the root if they can detect it, the shaman will go to the original cause, knowing that if this is resolved then the symptoms will fall away, just like a gardener understands that a weed will only die if its root ball is removed, and although Western medicine is extremely effective for acute and emergency issues such as traumatic injuries, surgeries or immediately life-threatening conditions, for slower and chronic long-lasting conditions authentic spiritual healing practices like shamanism and animism are, in my experience, much more effective. I believe many of the causes for chronic physical and mental issues are spiritual, and greatly benefit from more holistic forms of healing. For these conditions, just addressing the symptoms over and over again will only give minor and short-term relief, and often lead to other imbalances that are caused by the side effects from medication. This is where the benefit of what we in the West would call magical thinking comes into play. By beginning to understand the true nature of the world, that it is much vaster and more interconnected than we sense, we can start to see the interconnectedness of many issues that modern medicine cannot currently heal. By also developing our minds we can have a much greater understanding of our emotional capacity and how the mind can become a great tool when it comes to healing. Both of these things rely on an expansion of awareness and an openness to the possibility that there is more than our eyes can see and our hands can feel. Many people in the West come to spirituality through chronic mental or physical health conditions. I think this is because they are left with a 'last-resort mindset' as they have exhausted the options given to them by modern medicine, and believe they may as well give spirituality a try. This is exactly what happened to me, as I was faced with being told that I would never be able to live a life without anxiety unless I took medication, which came with its own issues. As I touched on at the start of this book, I did not come from a background that was openminded towards spiritual practice, but, feeling as though I had tried everything else, I gave it a go. When it started to actually work I couldn't believe it. If I am honest, if I hadn't been suffering, or if modern medicine could have rebalanced me, I probably would have never discovered spirituality, let alone shamanism. But the reality is that modern medicine could not offer me the help that I required. This is not down to the brainpower, financial constraints, lack of effort or well-meaning of those who work within modern medicine; it is simply down to differences in worldview and perception that cut the Western medical community off from spiritual realities and the interconnectedness of life. The overwhelming positive of allowing ourselves to magically think as Westerners is that we open ourselves up to the possibility of healing that which we have been told was unhealable. I have seen, time and time again, people recover from conditions that they were offered no hope for, such is the power of the healers of earth-centric spiritual cultures. But these traditional and indigenous cultures would not consider their worldview to be magical thinking. Their beliefs and wisdom have been shaped by thousands of years of trial and error, sacrifice and well-honed techniques that allow them to become far more sensitive than the average Westerner to the world around them. To them, they are not relying on blind faith or delusion, they are following the wisdom of their traditions that have served them well up to the modern day. The results of their work must also be verified by positive outcomes, or there is no use. Furthermore, what may seem unrelated in the West is very much interconnected in their view, and it is through the knowledge of this interconnectedness, and the clarity and wisdom derived from it, that they are able to offer such incredible healing to us.

The other really beneficial thing about traditional and indigenous spiritual concepts is that they assist them in remaining in balance with the natural world – something that we have unfortunately forgotten how to do. They understand the harm that comes from destroying habitat and unbalancing the energy of their local landscape, and so they make sure to remain as balanced as possible. This, I feel, is part of the reason that earth-centric cultures who are able to live in their traditional way, with their traditional landscape untouched, experience far less chronic physical and mental health issues than non-indigenous counterparts. If we look at our culture, the difference is striking, as our way of life depends on removing huge amounts of resources from the earth. We could never hope to balance this with the way that we live, so we must bear the consequences. Where traditional cultures see the world as more alive and *seem* to have fewer boundaries around their minds, ironically they have far more boundaries around their behaviour – which helps them to stay well and in balance. So, not only do earth-centric cultures carry the wisdom of healing, but they carry the wisdom of sickness prevention too. This means that a good deal of our sicknesses in the West could be avoided, and the results of them would be greatly reduced if we could begin to learn and apply traditional concepts to our own lives so we can start to alter our behaviour to come back to balance. This, though, may require some more openness to magical thinking.

But . . . while there are positives to magical thinking, it is not quite that simple.

THE NEGATIVES OF MAGICAL THINKING

Without a firm tradition that enables us to draw a line in the sand when we start opening up to spiritual practice (so that we have firm boundaries around what is possible and what isn't), we have no limits. Just because life isn't all that it may seem, it doesn't mean that anything is possible. This is a very important distinction that is often overlooked in the Western spiritual communities. In my personal journey, as I experienced feeling energy and the benefit that spiritual healing had on my mind and body, I discovered that there was another truth outside of the worldview of my upbringing. I knew that it wasn't all in my head, and I was really benefitting from it. But, due to the fact that at this point in my journey I had no idea about spiritual traditions, there were no limits to my magical thinking. Instead of expanding my boundaries of belief a healthy amount, with no guidance to do otherwise, I took this new-found truth to mean that everything I had ever been taught about life was a lie. This was not helpful, as it opened my mind up far too much and, after a while, nothing made any sense.

My head became filled with quotes such as:

'Think positive.'
'Spirit told me . . .'
'Believe and you will achieve.'
'Nothing is impossible.'
'We are all energy.'
'We are all one.'

You may have heard a few of these yourself. In fact, if you are into spirituality I'm sure you can fill in a few more. The problem with these quotes is that they lack the nuance required to really understand them. Nuances such as:

'Thinking positive will help, but it takes much more to undo many years of trauma.'

'If what you believe spirit is saying cannot be verified in everyday reality, don't worry about it.'

'Believing is not the only aspect of achieving – a huge amount of discipline and hard work is required.'

'Many things are impossible.'

'We are all energy, but I am a human having a human experience.'

'We are connected, but I am my own person, with my own boundaries, needs, wants and desires.'

Without these nuances, we can latch on to spiritual buzz-words that lead us away from the inner work that is needed before we can truly live and understand the meaning of these concepts. Without doing this, it's tempting to live in our heads and spend as much of our time away from reality as possible, for reality is painful. This is what is known as 'spiritual bypassing' – when we use spiritual ideas to dismiss or avoid dealing with the pain and difficulty of real life. To avoid this we must utilise spiritual practice to confront our issues in a slow, methodical and gentle way. To uncover them gently and come back to balance, rather than using spirituality to blast off into the cosmos and avoid our daily reality.

Mind projection is an incredibly powerful thing. When we project the inner workings of our mind onto the outside world, the results feel incredibly real, because they are real in our minds – the place that we process what we see in the outside world. If your mind really believes that something exterior represents something to you from your interior, that thing – whatever it is – will resemble whatever you project onto it. On one level, we have all done this. We can all think of when we meet somebody who reminds us of somebody else, and how – although they aren't that person – we project our memories of the original person onto them and it stimulates our emotions. Other forms of common magical thinking may be to not walk over three drains, or to knock on wood for good luck. On one level this is often normal and harmless, because we understand our mind's capacity for projection is tempered by our cultural viewpoints. But when we decide to leave the temperance of our cultural viewpoints behind, and instead mind projection is mixed with ungrounded forms of spiritual practice, we must be careful as we start opening up and becoming more sensitive to the world, as our minds can play havoc with all the new information we are bombarded with. It can leave us completely open, very impressionable, and easily manipulated by people who may sound like they know what they are talking about.

The best thing that we can do to guard ourselves against this risk is to follow a grounded form of spiritual practice that has its roots in the ancient past. Practices like shaman-ism allow us to be connected to knowledge and worldviews that have stood the test of time. This is so important. Spir-ituality is not about reinventing the wheel, but finding that peace within us that has always been there. While many New Age practices are focussed on ascension and what I call 'upward' forms of spirituality, shamanism helps us to go 'downward' and root firmly into the earth, which helps us to see with clarity. Our energy begins to circulate the body and not just the mind. This really helps us to stay in touch with reality when we embark on our spiritual healing journeys.

FINAL THOUGHTS ON MAGICAL THINKING

With magical thinking, we are all on the scale somewhere. If you feel that your worldview is limiting your joy and potential for healing, I encourage you to do some more research on earth-centric animist and shamanic cultures and practices, as they may have some answers for you. If you feel that you are becoming ungrounded due to your spiritual practice, perhaps it would help to give it a break and spend some time with people who will help bring you back down to earth, as well as connect to authentic earth-centric animist and shamanic traditions, as they can help to temper your mind projection and put it at rest. Both require a deep understanding of our own minds and how they work. If we understand our emotions then we can see the roots of our projection and pull back from them. Over time this helps us to see with clarity and wisdom. What is most important in spirituality, and our lives, is working towards a deeper understanding of the nature of reality. If we can do this, we can see and think clearly, engage with others confidently, and make decisions that lead us in the right direction. Too much, or not enough, magical thinking can lead us away from this centre point of balance, and that is why it is an important topic to speak about.

RITUAL 6

Air-Honouring Ritual

We share the air that we breathe with all things on this planet. Air is without borders, without identity, without stigma or opinion. Air is what connects life to life. The West is starting to understand the huge importance of air, with laws being made around pollution, and within the wellness space, with wonderful practices such as breathwork now becoming more and more available. People are learning that how and what we breathe is an essential part of our health, as well as the stabilising and balancing of our nervous system, which allows us to feel peaceful and calm and reduces the effects of stress.

But the air is much more than a combination of gases. Air is an animate force, alive, full of conscious energies.

This simple ritual is designed to offer something back to these forces, and to show gratitude to this essential part of life.

WHAT YOU NEED

- A pouch of offerings – grains/oats/seeds/ nuts
- Ethically sourced sacred herbs – mugwort/ sage/palo santo/juniper
- A lighter or matches

INSTRUCTIONS

- In the early morning make your way up to a hill with an unobstructed view of the four directions. If you live in an urban area and cannot do this, a window or balcony will do.

- At the top, light the sacred herbs and let the smoke waft in each of the four directions.
- As you do this, imagine this smoke feeding the energies of the wind in these directions.
- After this, take a handful of offerings and throw them high into the air in each direction.
- As you do this, offer your gratitude and thanks to the air and its forces.

Make sure to write your experiences in your shamanic journal including how you felt, and sensations in your body, or any other feelings that this ritual evoked upon you.

Just like an eagle soaring can offer a higher perspective and a further view than our normal range of vision, this ritual can bring a different, higher perspective on an issue, and help to create some space in your mind and a renewed sense of clarity.

You can perform this ritual as often as needed, but, as always, take care to do your best to integrate the lessons gleaned from previous rituals before you perform it again.

CHAPTER 7

Offerings – Communication
with the Land

In the last six chapters we have spoken about the process of initiation and healing from a psychological and spiritual perspective. We've chewed over the idea that perhaps our culture is not as spiritually void of power as it may first seem, and considered our innate human desire for connection and sense of belonging. This is one of the foundations of all spiritual practices in the world, and still leads us from tribe and family into community and then (hopefully) back to tribe. We have discussed the reality that New Age Western spiritual culture is mostly set up as a for-profit business and only benefits the few, not the many. As a remedy for this, we discussed the incredible importance of bringing spirituality into the mainstream and making it accessible and down-to-earth. We then journeyed together to the lands of myth and story, only to look down and realise that they were right at our feet all along, before debating the good and bad sides of magical thinking.

All of this is done with the aim to display the incredible beauty of traditional shamanic and animist viewpoints, and how we can strive to lay authentic versions of these practices in our own culture so that they can begin to aid us, and our future generations, in our own search for healing and returning into deeper relationship with the land.

So it is about time that we speak about the most important part of any earth-centric spiritual practice – offerings.

As humans we spend our lives making little holes in the fabric of life. That includes all of us, and even the most eco-conscious of communities must take care that they remain in balance. Nobody is perfect and we all must live somewhere and use natural resources to build homes, and burn fuel to stay warm and comfortable. Many of us rely on others hunting or killing animals for our nourishment. Even those who are plant-based must understand that farming practices result in the death of a myriad of animals. By our very existence, we contribute to the imbalance of nature. Life and death are two sides of the same coin, and because of this many animist and shamanic cultures believe that we are each born with a debt to the natural world.

To pay back this debt and repair some of the damage that humans create in the natural world, offerings are given. By giving specific offerings in auspicious places at auspicious times, these cultures signal to the spirit world their positive intentions, pay their respects to the spirits, and apologise for the imbalances that have been created.

These offerings also feed the spirits and keep them well nourished, so they do not look to those in the culture for retribution. Were this not to happen, the balance would not be kept, and eventually the damage would become too great to fix. This would result in too large an imbalance, and the forces that represent and protect the natural world would begin to bite back, which would start to detrimentally affect humans, making us sick. This idea of the ambivalence of the spirit world is a cross-cultural theme in all traditional earth-centric spiritualities. Although it is undoubtedly true that many traditional rituals are done for the honouring of loved and local deities to bring peace, abundance and joy, many are also performed out of the fear of what would happen if these spirits were to feel insulted due to lack of respect. Powerful energies can disrupt and cause harm to humans if they are not correctly acknowledged.

Offerings, then, are a particularly important concept to understand.

Offerings can be seen as the currency that is used between us and the spirit world. A ceremony without offerings would not only be seen as futile but also potentially dangerous, as the spirits being asked for assistance may get offended. Just like it is bad form to turn up at a friend's house empty-handed, entering a sacred space without some form of offering would not paint you in a very good light. And just like it is useful to grease somebody's palms a little if you want them to do you a favour, this also works well in the spirit world.

Alongside the fact that turning up on a spirit's doorstep with good intentions but no offerings won't get you very far, offerings also open up the lines of communication between the spirit world and us, generating positive spiritual energy and helping to dispel obstacles. They also show conviction in your spiritual practice and belief – which helps to generate good karma and positive conditions for your future.

In the simplest terms, an offering is something of tangible value that is given in order to appease and/or nourish a spirit. Often this could take the form of a plant that is burnt and produces a sweet scent – like juniper, sage or mugwort – or it could be a sweet resin – like copal or frankincense. These sacred smokes are said to carry the nourishing qualities of the plant or resin up to the spirits. (They are also said to clear the space of negative energies and spirits, but this is a different thing.)

Another common form of offering, particularly in nomadic shamanic cultures, is milk. This is the lifeblood of communities and forms a staple of the diet that allows indigenous nomads to survive the harsh landscape. Of course, it is not just nomads who have this relationship with milk. All mammals are raised on their mother's milk. A mother's ability to nourish her child is sacred, and milk is seen as pure and clean, and a perfect food for the spirits – some of which are human ancestor spirits who would have grown up on their mother's milk like many of us, and then fortified themselves on the milk of their herd throughout their lives. Interestingly, ancient accounts from Europe detail milk and honey as the preferred food offering for the fae – the fairy spirits of these lands. It is a sacred substance that allows life to flourish, and is a very potent offering. Fats derived from milk such as butter and ghee are also commonly used, particularly given to the fire where they produce a wonderful thick and powerful flame.

Tobacco is also a common offering that is used by shamanic and animist cultures of the Americas – such as the Wixárika, the First Nations tribes and those in the Amazon Basin. In the Americas, tobacco is seen as a master plant and a chief medicinal plant for spiritual healing – above even those with psychedelic qualities such as ayahuasca.

Another offering commonly given would be a type of grain. Similar to milk, grains are important staples of human life and sustain us. Barley, oats or corn are often offered to spirits.

These are what could be known as general offerings, and the above offerings are mostly the safest forms of offering for any spirit. An exception would be that it would not be a good idea to offer milk (or any other liquid) directly to the fire as it would dampen the flames or put it out altogether. Highly flammable liquids, or alcohol like vodka, are possible, but not ideal.

All of these offerings can be thrown in the air towards the sky and in the cardinal directions. They can be laid in auspicious places such as altars or spirit houses, or they can be placed and offered into the fire and burnt so that the spirits may feast on the smoke, or lit on fire and used accordingly (mugwort and sage for instance).

It is important to give your offering with conviction and heart and without doubt. Although doing so may feel strange at first, allow yourself to consider the possibility that what you are doing has great significance. Make sure to buy your offerings with money gained from meritorious actions and to not use money derived from crime or money that has come from the suffering of others.

Something that is especially important to note is what *not* to give as an offering. Although traditional cultures may also offer the blood of sacrificed animals, this is not an offering that should be given unless you know exactly which spirit you are looking to appease, and have a deep understanding of the shamanic practices you are working with. Many spirits do not enjoy the impurity of blood, and it could easily offend them if you sacrifice an animal on their behalf. It is also incredibly important not to give menstrual blood, or your own blood in other forms, as this is seen as insulting, and akin to urinating or defecating in a sacred space. Doing so can lead to injury, harm or even death from the spirits. This also includes urinating or defecating near rivers, springs or other natural water sources. Give what you cherish, or prize. Do not give waste products, or something that you would throw away were it not for giving it as an offering. A man who did one of my workshops started his offerings practice and, after a couple of weeks, he explained to the class that the place in nature that he had wanted to make a connection with had started to feel very hostile and unwelcome. Each time he went there he started to shiver and felt very unwelcome. He had not followed the instructions given and was offering all of his food waste! This was no doubt angering the spirits of that place and they were letting him know it. He got off quite lightly!

The practice of offerings is a huge leap of faith for a Westerner. Although we will gladly give presents to each other, and even our beloved pets, to give something of tangible value to a spirit seems like madness. I understand this way of thinking, as I was the same. When I was instructed to give my first offering it felt very bizarre. I didn't really have any concept about what a spirit was, and I definitely didn't know what to expect if I met one, but I decided to give it a go, so I tentatively strolled into the local park with a bag of apples. A big oak loomed in the distance, and I thought I had nothing to lose by trying. Kneeling in front of the tree, I called out to its spirit – whoever it was – introduced myself and explained that I was only there to give it some respect, that I didn't want anything in return, and that I was sorry if I was interrupting it. I thought of the spirit as a Godfather-type character. Someone that would probably like some honouring but didn't want any small talk. I lay the apples down and mumbled my prayer – something about how beautiful the oak was, and how these apples were organic and how much my ancestors would have enjoyed them. Nothing happened, of course, so I looked around to see if anybody had seen what I had done and quickly got out of there, feeling a little embarrassed at the fact I had just spoken to a tree for a few minutes and given it some apples. I do understand the irony of giving apples to a tree, but I didn't have anything else! Over time I returned to that same tree with other offerings – nuts, oats, flowers. Each time I introduced myself and then lay the offerings down and gave my wishes and honouring to the tree. It was very DIY and a little chaotic. This was in the early days and I was figuring it out as I went along – which isn't recommended, but I didn't have much choice. After a few weeks, I observed that the immediate area around the oak tree started to feel more alive whenever I went there. It's hard to describe other than saying it seemed to recognise me. The rest of the park was the same as it had always been, but the area around the tree itself started to take on a new vibrancy. It was as if it was responding to me going each week and feeding it with prayers and offerings. I am pretty cynical, and I tried to chalk it up to the placebo effect, but I couldn't ignore the feeling of connectedness that it brought me. I then started to dream about the place.

AXIS MUNDI

In shamanic cultures there is a concept of the axis mundi. This is an 'entry point' to the otherworlds, and when undertaking a spirit journey in trance, some shamans utilise this axis mundi as a gateway to enter and exit the spirit world. Often this axis mundi is represented by a landmark, or tree, that connects this world to the heavens and/or the worlds below this earth, and a relationship to this axis mundi can provide a shaman with great power and healing capabilities. We have already discussed how traditional earth-centric cultures base their spirituality around their local area, and this axis mundi is often the centre of the world for these cultures and a place where they believe the world began for them, and sometimes where it will end. The Black Hills for the Sioux or Mount Kailash in Tibet are examples of natural landmarks that hold great meaning for their cultures. An axis mundi is sometimes travelled into spiritually by the shaman during trance, so that they are able to gain the knowledge and wisdom needed to assist their people. In the ancient animist Norse tradition from Northern Europe, it is said that Odin travelled down the roots of Yggdrasil (a giant ash or yew tree that supported and unified all nine worlds in Norse cosmology). Part of Yggdrasil was said to emerge from a deep well that held all of the secrets and power of the universe. This was Mimir's well (Mimisbrunnr), and the God who presided over it, Mimir, held the wisdom that Odin desired. Odin, understanding that he must offer something of great importance to him, offered his own eye to Mimir for one sip of the well's water. This offering was accepted and Odin was allowed his sip – bestowing him with great power. But this was not enough, and in order to learn more and satiate his yearning for knowledge and foresight, he impaled himself on his own spear amongst the branches above the well for nine days and nights, entering the trance state between life and death. It was during this ultimate offering – of himself – that he ultimately gained a glimpse of the runes, and with an almighty scream he scooped them up and gained the endless wisdom he had been seeking. This myth shows the great importance of offering and sacrifice, and what we must do in order to work with and gain favour from the numinous. It also details a common theme in shamanic initiation, which is for the initiate to be destroyed and then reconstituted and symbolically brought back to life by the spirits, imbued with new wisdom and clarity.

This idea of the world tree is taught in Western core shamanism and was what inspired me to start giving offerings to the tree near my home. While I didn't gouge out my own eye or impale myself in the park, making a commitment to return weekly and give my offerings and prayers to the spirit of the tree in my own way was a small reflection of these ancient shamanic practices.

That tree would become a place that I would go back to when I was feeling energetically depleted, and during my healing and ceremonies it was where I journeyed into the otherworlds to converse with spirit. Over time, it started to hold great meaning and power for me. By giving these offerings I slowly started to learn how to commune with the spirit world. Although when I began, I didn't yet have any firm concepts of what a spirit was, or the different types, this offering process started to teach me to feel when a place was responding to me, and when it wasn't.

It took many years to develop and master a proper offerings practice, but the effects didn't take long to manifest in the beginning. In my one-to-one practice I have many success stories from introducing people to this process. A very welcome byproduct is the grounding that it brings, and if you suffer from mental health issues then an offerings practice is a very potent way to alleviate some of the pressure and negative self-talk that exists in many of our heads. An important side note here is to not project too much magical thinking onto the process and make it as hands-on as possible. Giving offerings puts us in a state of reciprocity and allows us to feel gratitude for what we have, instead of lamenting what we don't have – this encourages a more positive outlook on the world. During healings or retreats, I would encourage participants to go out onto the land, to a place that they were drawn to. Once there I would tell them to introduce themselves and leave an offering – along with a prayer of thanks for what they have in their lives. I would ask them to do this each morning, or when they felt ungrounded. When I would ask people how they felt after this, they would say that they felt a renewed sense of recognition for the world around them, and they felt the interconnected nature of life as the place they were feeding responded to them. Many also said that they felt a huge weight could be lifted off their shoulders by petitioning the higher powers for help. This is really the foundational aspect of shamanism, and it is through offerings that we start to develop lived experience of it.

Traditional cultures have always appealed to higher powers to assist with their lives on earth, which were always difficult, and it is a beautiful thing to be able to remind somebody who grew up in the modern world about the option of this spiritual assistance. The effect of faith in higher powers that are looking out for us is actually quite miraculous, and for many people a missing piece to the puzzle of their healing. But as is so often the case in earth-centric practice, what makes this effective is the combining of the numinous with practicality – e.g. getting your boots on, clambering through the mud and into the woods to a specific place, and then physically giving an offering to a place. It's important we don't just use our heads in spiritual practice, and adding some physical exertion makes this very grounding as it allows a person to integrate the experience into their bodies as well as their minds. Just like Odin didn't just *think* about Mimir's well and all the knowledge that it held, he physically travelled, offered what he could and lived through the struggle of the experience – sometimes we must, in our own way, make spirituality more tangible.

In our modern lives, it is so easy to live a life of distraction and get so caught up in our heads that we forget to look up and take into account the wonder of the natural world and its ability to provide for us. Although we may live lives that seem so disconnected from the natural rhythm of life, it doesn't take too much to remind ourselves that at our core we are the same humans that we have always been. Offerings can be a wonderful way that we start to settle back into the natural pace of life, which naturally calms down the mind. A combination of the humility, practicality and the reciprocal nature of giving offerings helps the internal maelstrom of the mind to realign itself into a natural order. As humans we are not meant to have chaotic minds. This is a symptom of imbalance, which often stems from an imbalance in our local surroundings. Offerings settle our own minds as they repair the damage of the natural world and allow us to *feel* – not just imagine – the natural interconnectedness of life. As already spoken about in this book, this idea is easy to grasp intellectually, but embodying interconnectedness is much more difficult. Offerings help us to understand that the individual pain that we feel is the *same* collective pain that the land feels. As *part* of life, we are intrinsically connected to the natural world and to the spirits that live there. The separation that we feel is due to our own minds and is false. Just like a baby who is connected by the umbilical cord to its mother shares her health, we are only as healthy as our local surroundings. We start to heal individually by nourishing the earth, and we do this through offerings. Over time, we realise that our pain is not as personal as we think, and that we don't have to have the entire world on our shoulders.

RITUAL 7

Begin an Offerings Practice

I invite you to begin your own practice of giving offerings.

Traditional cultures all have very well-developed offerings practices, which link up to the complex subject of astrology. Certain offerings are given to certain spirits at certain times. This book is designed as an introduction to earth-based spiritual practice and does not go into the depth that a traditional lineage would. The most important thing is to stay safe.

Avoid giving offerings to water sources, as the spirits there can carry a different energy. Choose a tree far away from any burial grounds or mounds, or sacred sites. A small section of trees in a small woodland is ideal. We are not looking to save the world or make huge changes to the world, but instead to start slowly and gently, coming into relationship with the world around us.

The first thing to make sure of is that you maintain an awareness of a key concept of offerings: leave the natural world better off than it was when you found it. It can be tempting as humans to want to do something big – to create a huge offering to affirm our huge affection for the spirit world and nature. However well intentioned this may be, the issue is that without a complex understanding of the spirit world, going 'too big' with an offering can disturb nature rather than feed it. Therefore I advise against this, and instead implore you to go about this as humbly as possible.

A small handful of grain is more than enough.

After you have your chosen offering, place it in a small bag and get out into nature.

It helps if this place is near where you live, as to really form a relationship with a place it is best to be able to return at least semi-regularly.

When you are walking, leave your phone, or any other device in your pocket. Don't listen to music or a podcast on your headphones and instead take this time to tune in to the natural rhythm of life. Treat the entire process as a sort of meditation. Notice the movement of the birds, the squirrels or other creatures. Take in the scents of the flowers and the damp soil.

Which way is the wind blowing through the trees?

It is easy to forget in our busy day-to-day that the natural world is in constant motion. It never stops - never slows down, or speeds up. It just is.

If this is your first time, as you are walking, focus on something constant. This could be your breathing, or your footsteps as they crunch on the ground. Allow your senses to calm and tune yourself into your local environment.

Repeat this intention in your mind three times:

'Which place is calling me?'

Allow the natural landscape to draw you towards a point of attention. Following the advice from this chapter, allow yourself to be drawn towards a tree.

Approach the tree slowly and humbly. It is important that you do the next part with faith, conviction and heart. Release doubt for the next few moments, and allow yourself to consider the possibility that what you are doing has great importance.

Bow your head and kneel, introducing yourself and your intention for your offering.

Compliment the tree and the local landscape – allow your words to be as poetic as possible. Do all of this out loud.

Once your prayer is completed, lay the offering and bow your head once again, backing away from the tree slowly and then turning around and walking home.

It is important not to ask for anything, and to simply give out of honouring for what you have in your life.

CHAPTER 8

Ancient Wisdom with a Modern Mindset – Shamanism and the Community

One of the great difficulties of healing is integrating the lessons we have learnt. Shamanic methods are incredibly powerful, and the speed in which they can address our issues can be difficult for the rational mind to come to terms with. For some people this can make the whole experience quite discombobulating. This is particularly true when it comes to mental health conditions, as when the root of these conditions has been soothed the outward symptoms of anxiety or OCD may still exist for a period of time. If our minds have been fixed into thinking a certain way for many years, it is normal that this doesn't simply change overnight. We need to take care and time and learn to 'rehab' ourselves to a newer, lighter and more free way of thinking. This is a process that takes lots of trust, commitment and often assistance from others.

Part of the reason that shamanism is so effective in

traditional cultures, such as those in Central Asia, or Central or South America, is that they exist within a cultural setting that supports this way of healing. When a person goes to see a shaman they understand the concepts that the shaman is working with and, just like when we go to see a doctor, there is a level of comfort and ease in the way that they work because they have grown up with it. Due to this level of cultural acceptance with the practice, when the shaman performs a healing or ceremony it is all very normal. Just like we trust our Western doctors to heal us, and trust that following their advice and their allopathic methods means that we will get better in time, those in traditional cultures do the same with their healers.

In my experience, a shamanic healing, or ceremony, can feel like an astonishingly alien experience to a Westerner. The thumping of the drums, the searing rattles or throng of the jaw harp, combined with monotonous and droning prayers and chants while sweet smoke rises up from the offerings in the fire and envelopes the room. Huge amounts of energy are generated and the shamans' energy courses through a person's body as their sickness is located, diagnosed and 'knocked' out of them. You may feel the spirits a shaman works with arrive in the room, hear footsteps and feel their hands upon you. Many people start to shake as they release huge amounts of tension. There may be tears, or hysterical laughter. A person may see a huge array of visions for the first time in their life. When I first sat in on a ceremony performed for people in a traditional setting, by a traditional shaman, I was scared stiff, as the power that the shaman was generating was quite overwhelming for me, but the locals were very relaxed, scrolling through their Facebook feeds and generally just relaxing as if they were at a family gathering. At first I was surprised at how normal they thought it all was, but it really taught me that we can be much more authentic and grounded with sacred space in the West. We often sit bolt upright, dressed in white and with a very holier-than-thou attitude. While there are protocols to follow so we do not offend the shaman and the spirits – it is more than okay to relax too! But regardless of whether you are able to relax or not, you are taken on a real journey, and when you land you very well may be a different person. You may leave feeling a sense of clarity and renewed power that feels both brand new but incredibly familiar. This may last days, weeks or months. But eventually, the ecstasy of a shamanic ritual begins to fade and we must get back in amongst the mundane world.

I found this incredibly challenging during my first shamanic training in the UK. For three years we would meet together deep in the woods for four days of very intense ceremony multiple times a year. It would be deep, raw and very moving – and then on Sunday evenings I would pack up my tent, jump in my car and make my way back into the world. Nothing quite brings you back from life-changing spiritual experiences like a service station cheese sandwich and bumper-to-bumper traffic on the M25 as you crawl past Heathrow Terminal 5. At 6 am on Monday my alarm would go off and I would drag myself out of bed, bleary-eyed, get ready for work, and jump on the train at rush hour.

The training was the first time in my life that I really experienced the magic of sacred space fully, and the effortless connection and heart-opening emotions that arose with it. Each time I had to leave I felt despair in having to trudge back to my ordinary life. When I would arrive back at work on Monday morning after a block of my training, I would have a sense of entitlement and would chastise my colleagues for getting so worked up about things that I believed were trivial. I had been doing *really* important work like healing myself, sitting in ceremony, and giving offerings to the land – so in my naivety this gave me permission to roll my eyes into the back of my head when I read email threads about meaningless drivel such as 'Who wasted all the printer ink?' or 'Please don't be five minutes late again.'

Unbeknownst to me at the time, I had fallen into one of the great traps of spiritual work, which is to assume that you are above those who are not on the same path. This went on for a good while, until, within a ceremony, I received the message loud and clear – what real worth was my spiritual practice if I was becoming more and more separated from my colleagues and more and more unable to function in the everyday world? I felt ashamed, as I saw how I had been acting from a higher perspective. It was not for me to decide what was trivial and meaningless, and it was incredibly arrogant of me to believe that my week-end spiritual work was in any way worth more than a colleague who was working very hard in a nine-to-five to support their family.

I knew I had to bring a sense of earthiness and disci-pline to my practice, and this came from a very potent plant medicine ceremony with the Wixárika. I would usu-ally drive to their local gatherings whenever they were in and around London and arrive about an hour before the ceremony began. This way everything was already set up and all I would have to do was get changed, grab a cushion and my sleeping bag and find a place in the circle and wait for the mara'akame (shaman) to signal that we would be starting. I didn't really like the waiting around and making small talk, so I tried to time it as close to the start point as possible. One evening I arrived at my normal time and got changed. Just as I locked my car and started walking down to the ceremonial tipi, a huge growl of thunder rattled the sky and the heavens opened up, sending heavy torrential rain down directly on top of us. The tipi had been put up at the bottom of a valley, and in the time it took me to walk a few minutes down the hill, the ground had already become sodden and waterlogged and resembled more of a swamp than the quaint flower meadow it had been a few moments earlier. As I got closer, a thick-set Colombian man handed me a shovel. He was the firekeeper (the person who would make sure the fire was always lit and never went out throughout the all-night ceremony), and before I could say anything he motioned to me that I had to dig a trench around the tipi so that the water would drain instead of seeping in under the sides and ruining the ceremony – which it had already started to do. This was a matter of urgency, as once a ceremony has been planned it must go ahead at all costs. I wasn't about to say no, and I took that shovel and went to work. Within minutes I was drenched, but after digging as quickly as I could after an hour we had salvaged the ceremony. Just as the ceremony was starting to begin, I entered the tipi, absolutely soaked to the bone, freezing, with red-raw hands and caked with mud from head to toe.

A Wixárika peyote ceremony lasts all night, from sunset to sunrise. They begin with the mara'akame 'singing down' the sun and then finish with the last song that sings it back up again. There are five songs in total throughout the night, and these songs track the movements of the sun on the other side of the world and honour the sacred powers and sacred sites of the Wixárika people. It's an incredibly beautiful experience and, when combined with the magical chanting of the mara'akame, the peyote cactus is a very healing medicine. But these sorts of ceremonies are long and arduous, emotional and difficult at the best of times. The thought of having to sit all night long soaking wet was kicking up a lot of resistance for me. I had always come to these ceremonies with very well-defined intentions in order to get the most out of it. This time I was so cold and uncomfortable that I couldn't focus and it was really bothering me. I was called up to take my first dose of the bitter medicine and returned to my cushion, in a sulk. Slowly, as the ceremony began and the peyote slowly started to scan my body and work out the kinks, I started to relax a little bit. Many people also thanked me for digging the trench, including the man who was sponsoring the ceremony, which was something I didn't realise would happen. As I looked down on my blistered hands I felt a sense of pride for what I had done, and it felt really good to be appreciated for being an important part of the evening. The night wound on, and as the fire started to dry my clothes and warm my skin, I looked around at people laughing, crying and praying deeply for happiness and joy in their lives. A flower started to blossom in my heart, and very slowly an overwhelming feeling of gratefulness began to bubble up inside me. I stared at the beautiful fire, so thankful for its gentle warmth, and realised that I had been missing the point of shamanic ceremony up until this moment. It dawned on me that previously I had spent a lot of the ceremonies in my head. Ruminating over thoughts and patterns and memories and traumas. This didn't really ever get me anywhere, for every breakthrough was followed by another memory and trauma, or another reason to be anxious or upset. This had prevented me from really being present and feeling part of the ceremony and the community. I had been on my own journey, instead of connected to the communal ceremony that I was partaking in with the rest of the people there. This became the most healing medicine ceremony of my life, and it was all because I was handed that shovel and told to dig. It was the first night that I was able to get out of my head and into my (shivering) body. I had, for the first time, offered my physicality to the spirits and the community instead of my mind. The discomfort at the start had forced me to forget about all the complex mind stuff and surrender. As the fire flickered and danced in the darkness, and in the midst of this revelation, I understood that we must do our best to remember that shamanic work is not just a psychotherapeutic model of healing. If we see it this way, we miss out on so much of the power that is generated through the ceremony. Much of the healing of the mind that we experience through shamanism is a byproduct of learning to surrender to the healing process and allow the mysterious healing powers of the land, the elements and the spirits to flow through us. This starts to shrink our individual neuroses as we begin to realise that what we crave is not necessarily the one magic answer to all of our problems, but a sense of connection to something deep enough that allows us to feel safe despite them. This is how we let healing happen. Shamanic work has not really made any of my issues go away, but it has allowed me to grow my sense of awareness to a size that many of them now feel non-existent.

This is the great power of shamanism, I think, and why it is so effective for Westerners. It is a spiritual practice of *inclusion*, where we are able to find a safe home for *all* aspects of ourselves. This is such an important concept for healing, and why so many end up tripping themselves up on their healing journeys as they spend so much energy in trying to find ways to cut parts of themselves off, hoping then to only be left with the parts that make them feel good. But all this does is make us focus on our perceived inadequacies. There is a sense of deep peace and relaxation in coming to the realisation that we don't need to relentlessly analyse all our issues or insecurities to heal them. Shamanism provides a platform that allows us to become in service to powers greater than ourselves – our community, the land or our traditions. This creates an *expansion* where our issues begin to feel smaller – we feel how insignificant they are as we slowly reconnect to the wider world and our sacred purpose within it.

This experience with the shovel really taught me about the balance between physical, or 'earthly', work and spiritual healing. 'Practise' means 'to put into action' and, although many people are drawn to healing through the desire to understand the nature of their minds – which is important – spirituality is not just about being in your head all the time. On my retreats, we laugh that 'retreat' is probably the wrong word to use. They definitely aren't five-star retreats with green juices and athleisure (although these are nice too). Instead, each of the participants sleep in a field together and, on top of the difficult and challenging nature of the ceremonies, they are also given a physical job to be responsible for, which is chosen according to their personalities. This could be digging holes, chopping wood, washing and carrying rocks for the ceremonial saunas, or assisting in decorating the altars. People also wash their own dishes and put their own cups away. This might seem trivial (or like I'm just trying to save money!) but the whole ethos of the retreat is that we are getting together in a community for several days. We all eat, dream, dance, sweat, argue, shout, laugh, cry and heal together. On the surface, adding even more work to the participants' plates when they have all come with their own separate issues to heal may seem as if it makes the entire process more difficult for them. It may even seem a little cruel. But when we receive feedback from the participants, the fact that they had this extracurricular work was one of the most moving parts of the entire experience for them. The Western mind *loves* to run wild with thoughts and ideas. In our culture this has brought us many wonderful things, but on a healing journey there is a tendency to inflate our issues to the point where they become overwhelming. By adding physical and earthly work to the sacredness of the retreat space the participants are able to step out of their minds and into their bodies. This helps their psychological processes settle, and acts as a type of grounding meditation. Also, just like digging the ditch helped back when I was learning to feel part of the ceremony, all participants feel that they have lent a physical hand in creating the ceremonial space on these retreats. Sweating in the ceremonial sauna, for example, is much more powerful for people who had a physical hand in building the actual structure, which is a womb-like structure created by long, thin hazel poles that are lashed together with pieces of rope in a dome that we all build together. The participants are also invited to say a personal prayer as they tie the poles – this way, the structure literally becomes a house of their own prayers. To step inside this structure all together in the pitch-black night, after dancing around a fire for hours, becomes a very moving and healing experience. Getting to the end of the ceremony when your feet hurt, your hands are blistered, your back aches and sweat pours off your body adds counterweight to the buoyancy of the deep and ethereal soul work that has been achieved. With this balance a sense of gratitude for all aspects of life follows.

Another thing that can make the healing journey far easier is if your journey is recognised by those in your life. In many animist and shamanic communities, when a person is in a spiritual crisis people understand the signs and symptoms, and when a person undertakes spiritual healing they are supported throughout the process. When a person goes through an initiation, which as explained in Chapter 1 is a form of healing journey, the initiate is welcomed back into the community with open arms. To assist them in integrating their healing they are often given a different role within that community so that they can 'live' their healing. For example, a trainee shaman that I met from the Wixárika had just been given the role of lawmaker or 'sheriff' for five years as part of his duties. For five years it was his job to note down all of the wrongdoings of his people so that they could then be held accountable and cleansed by the fire spirit – Tatewari. This cultural recognition supports the individual's spiritual journey and helps them to ground the psychological changes and growth in the everyday. This way, their external life (identity and purpose) is able to grow at the same speed as their internal life (the soul). Within certain First Nations cultures, such as the Sioux, Blackfoot and Cree, a vision quest is a ceremony of initiation. The initiate will go and sit on a hill for four days and four nights, without food or water, and will call or 'cry' to the spirits for a vision. After the four days and nights are completed, they will go back down to their elders and relay their experience to them. The elders will then decide amongst themselves what this experience means for the initiate. The initiate will potentially receive a new name and a new role when they are integrated back into the community, who are waiting for them and understand exactly what they have been doing. The entire community understands that a great change has occurred and that this person is now different to who they were when they left a few days prior. In other cultures, such as the animist Tz'utujil Maya, an initiate may receive new colours of clothing after their initiation rites, which they wear upon returning to their community. I have also read that some initiates are taught new subsets of their language, only known to those who have also undertaken the same initiation. Upon hearing a person speaking this dialect the rest of the community understand what this person has been through and acknowledge them accordingly.

This is a far cry from our modern society, where unfortunately the reality of the spiritual healing process is not part of the mainstream. While the tide is turning and people are becoming much more interested in practices such as shamanism, there is still not much mainstream support around those who experience either a spiritual crisis or undertake a journey of spiritual healing and growth. A regular occurrence at the end of our shamanic retreats was that a participant would explain they felt brand new, much lighter and that they couldn't wait to take their new sense of personal empowerment back into the world. Often I would get an email around six months later from some of the participants, explaining that this feeling had slowly begun to slip from their grasp and they felt as if they were back to square one. As mentioned in Chapter 2, ceremony and shamanic healing opens a window of opportunity where real change can occur. The wounds of the soul can be nourished, and we have a chance to move forward – often against the odds. But just like a drug addict cannot go back to drugs if they want to stay clean, each person must stop putting themselves in situations that contributed to their sickness if they don't want it to return. If we slip back into the conditions that caused or supported our sickness in the first place, and keep up with negative habits, then before long our healing initiations become misty memories of magic, almost like they never really happened, and we need to start the process again. This is the part of the healing process where we need grit and determination. Away from the ceremonial space and back in our everyday lives, where there is temptation around each corner. Healers can do many things, but they cannot walk for us.

The uncomfortable truth is that we must all learn the difficult process of knowing when to move on if our healing is untenable due to those around us not honouring the change that is occurring within us – even if it is just temporarily while we integrate a new way of being that supports us in flourishing and living peacefully. Those on the retreats who had more support from their home and work environments seemed to be able to integrate the changes into their lives much easier than those whose home or work life was too rigid to support growth. This points towards the importance of community-wide support when it comes to healing. If we lived in a society that understood the concepts and capacity of shamanic healing, and provided the support for people to go on these incredibly powerful healing journeys, then it would make the process much easier. A society where, when a person makes their triumphant return, they are given a new role, new responsibilities, new titles or even a new name. This may seem like a pipe dream, but this is exactly what happens in our society today when people achieve a milestone in education or work. When a person becomes a doctor they are addressed as such. When somebody completes university they are given a graduation certificate at a ceremony, which includes a traditional dress code and ritualistic elements (throwing the hats into the air to signal completion of this cycle). Through this recognition they then *elevate* their status and are able to access roles within culture that they previously would not have been able to. To transfer this to spirituality is a matter of communicating the importance of the spiritual journey to as many people as possible, and then integrating the concepts into our society over time. My view is that a person who has been on a true healing journey is of just as great a use to our society as a person who achieves an academic title. These should both be recognised as they both allow a deeper wisdom to feed back into our culture at large, which assists in renewing it (as we spoke about in Chapter 4).

The most inspiring people to me are those who have been through the difficult periods of healing, the retreats, or other similar initiatory healing events, and found ways to bring their healing back to their communities and families. While this book is about shamanism in the modern world, you definitely do not need to be a shaman to make a huge difference to others. Many people from our retreats, or my one-to-one sessions, go on to set up incredible initiatives, men's groups, women's groups and other community-minded programmes in order to support people in their local communities. By learning core shamanic concepts and looking to indigenous cultures for inspiration they have learnt to incorporate grounded and authentic wisdom into our society. These communities can be what I call 'shamanically minded' without necessarily being full-on hardcore shamanic traditions, which will undoubtedly come with time as more and more people become aware of this way of healing.

RITUAL 8

Earth-Honouring Ritual

We have now created an altar in our home, learnt how to honour the sacred directions, and paid our respects to the fire, the water, the air and our families. It is now time to pay something back to this wonderful earth.

A beautiful way to do this is to plant a seed in a sacred manner. Throughout time, cultures from around the world have partaken in sacred ceremonies to ensure that their crops will grow well each year. Although in the West we have lost these rites, we can still remind ourselves of the importance of paying our graces to the natural world and its cycles.

If you have a garden, you can plant a yearly fruiting seed in a suitable location, but you can also plant a small flowering plant indoors if you do not have access to a garden.

WHAT YOU NEED

- A suitable location (pot or soil) for a seed to thrive (do your research according to the plant you choose).
- Access to a water source to nourish the plant when it is needed.
- Adequate time to look after the plant.
- A pre-written and memorised poem or song directed at the earth, the seed and the plant. This could include examples of your gratefulness to the earth, your wonder at its beauty, your thanks to your ancestors who planted seeds so your family could thrive, or anything else that you feel in your heart.

INSTRUCTIONS

- Plan to plant your seed according to the best time of year for your plant (do some research to find this out).
- Prepare the soil, or pot, mindfully – each movement being a sacred and conscious act.

- When you plant the seed, recite your pre-written and memorised poem or song. Focus your attention on the soil (earth), the seed and the plant. You can use the rattle from the fire ceremony to focus your attention if you like.
- Tend to your plant when needed. If your plant flowers, you can put it next to your altar.
- Treat this plant with sacred reverence.

CHAPTER 9

A Spirituality to Balance the World

If we are going to find a way to embed earth-centric spiritual practices like animism and shamanism into the modern world, then we need a mythology to base them around that appeals to the majority, not the minority. Although I have dedicated my life to shamanism for nearly the last decade, I am not under any false pretence that the majority are able to devote their lives to this practice. I also do not think that there is one form of worship that applies to everyone, everywhere.

But there is a deeper issue at play in the West since the fall of mainstream religion and worship. Without something deep and meaningful to bring us together, we look for other, more transient forms of identity that inevitably end up driving us apart. In the modern West there is currently a huge divide between the right and left wing of politics. Gender identity disagreements are also causing the breakdown of families and tribe, and wars continue to break out due to the squabbles of isolated and immature, but powerful, men. Social media apps stoke these fires, reducing complex personal beliefs and identities into bite-size and simplified pieces of content, forcing a lack of nuance and urging bluntness and scandal for a few more shares and likes. As a society, we are growing further and further apart, and further away from what really matters. Amongst this, the world – with no care for opinion or fence-sitting – bubbles and boils, and refugees are wrenched from their homes and scattered across the world, looking for care and compassion to soothe wounds that most of us could only imagine.

This increasing distance between us all is ironic: since the internet was birthed on 1 January 1983 the world has become increasingly connected. But as our online connectivity has grown, and the lines between cultures have started to blur, we are now finding ourselves increasingly disconnected from the natural world and each other. It often feels like the world has become all about opinion and ego, and the projection of unresolved inner tension. It is suddenly not okay to just accept our differences, and in the search for truth people do what they have always done – they pick sides. While this is not a new phenomenon, due to the internet it is perhaps playing out on a global scale for the first time, and life is starting to get messy because of it. It happened a lot during the pandemic, as the anti-vax, anti-lockdown and anti-mainstream medicine communities clashed with their opposing sides – who were often people who were in their own families and friendship circles. For nearly three years, it seemed as though the entire world was divided. This was fascinating, as all both sides wanted was the exact same thing – which was to return to normality.

Ultimately, if we want our society to come together we cannot keep highlighting our differences. Instead, without sounding like a preacher, it seems as though – if we are going to now come together and move forward as a global culture – we must unite under a common theme. Logically this is that we are all caretakers for this earth, which is the one thing that binds us all together, no matter where we come from or believe, for despite what some may hope, there is only one planet that we can call home. This wonderful, beautiful, miracle of an earth. She is the mother that we all share, which makes us all family. The Lakota end their prayers to her with a moving reminder of this, ever reminding us of our interconnectedness: 'Mitakuye Oyasin' – 'We are all related.'

As global warming and climate change looms ever closer, we must change our ways and learn to live in balance, together. It is here that earth-centric forms of worship such as animism and shamanism can assist us greatly. Although comprising just 5 per cent of the world's population, indigenous people who still follow animist or shamanic belief successfully steward 80 per cent of the planet's biodiversity. They are experts in the nurture and conservation of the natural world, and this is, in a large way, due to their spiritual beliefs. By seeing the world around them as spiritually alive and part of their wider family they take great care in making sure that they remain in balance and in good relationship with it, never taking more than they need, which allows for the regeneration of fauna and flora. As Chapter 7, on offerings, also explained, alongside this practical behaviour, in a spiritual sense the natural world is renewed and replenished in the face of human-made imbalances by the feeding and nourishing of the spirits that represent it. If we were to lose earth-centric forms of worship, it would have dire consequences for humankind. If the people of the Amazon, for example, were to lose their spiritual beliefs and begin to see the forest as spiritually void, offering nothing beyond financial gain, the selling off of the flora and fauna and resulting land clearing would release up to 120 billion metric tonnes of carbon – equivalent to twelve years of global emissions. This would push global climate change well over safe limits. Instead, their shamanic beliefs and traditions teach them that nothing is worth more than their land, and this inspires them to fight for it, which luckily for us has greatly assisted in, so far, keeping the world in a salvageable state for humanity. But this dedication to their practices not only protects the rainforests – their teachings emanate outward to the West and teach us how we can also come into balance with nature. This is now starting to occur all over the world, as traditional cultures from Asia, Central and North America, Africa and Australasia have begun sharing their authentic and sacred teachings with the West, helping us to change our lives and live in a more sustainable, peaceful way. If this is the effect of just a fraction of the world's population following an earth-centric way of worship, one can imagine the hugely positive outcomes as more of us begin living with similar belief systems.

Arguably the most well-known polytheistic and animist society from Europe were the Ancient Greeks. To this day we take great lessons from their philosophers and astrological, medicinal and technological advancements. But just as meaningful for our modern lives are their myths. In Chapter 5 we spoke at length about the beauty that myth has to transcend time and space – to make the personal collective and vice versa. Myth amplifies the personal to a level that we can stand back gazing at it in awe, or drop to our knees and beg for its mercy. Especially apt for this chapter, I feel, is the Ancient Greek myth of Erysichthon and the goddess Demeter. The Ancient Greeks worshipped gods and goddesses who each had their own personalities, desires and fears. The deities, considered much more powerful than humans, were honoured and revered at certain times of the year for certain reasons – to bring the harvest, the rain or good luck in battle. The Ancient Greeks also believed in omens, and worshipped natural phenomena like groves, rivers and trees, as they also believed that nature was imbued with powerful spirits. There are even accounts of priestesses who descended into trance states to channel deities, particularly in the cult of Dionysus – the God of wine, theatre and madness. Unfortunately too little is known about this part of Ancient Greek worship to say whether it is shamanic or not, but one thing is certain – their practices were earth-centric and very similar to shamanic cultures that we see in the world today. This is interesting, as this demonstrates how many of the foundations of our modern society hail from animistic cultures.

The goddess Demeter was goddess of the harvest, who presided over the fields and crops of the Ancient Greeks. This, clearly, was very important, as without successful harvests an agrarian culture such as the Ancient Greeks would have ceased to exist at all, and in peacetime 80 per cent of their population devoted themselves to crop and field.

King Erysichthon was the King of Thessaly. Within his kingdom lay a grove that was sacred, and it belonged to the goddess Demeter. This particular grove was unrivalled in its beauty. Dryads (forest spirits) frolicked amongst the sweet scents of fruiting trees, and all manner of sacred worship occurred there. It was said that in this grove every sort of animal and tree co-existed in harmonious revelry, and abundance prevailed throughout the year. In the centre of this grove grew the goddess Demeter's tree – a towering and thick oak, lush with leaves and acorns, with boundless branches that provided cool shade to all those who came with respect and heartfelt honouring for the goddess.

King Erysichthon decided that this would be a beautiful place for a new feasting hall, and he mustered his men and ordered them to set about making that a reality. One by one the trees were felled by the razor-sharp axes of Erysichthon's men, until at last the goddess Demeter's oak trembled and crashed to the ground. The goddess, seeing the destruction of her grove, came in disguise to dissuade the greedy king from continuing, warning him that if he proceeded in destroying the grove he would face severe punishment. In his lust for a new hall to satiate his ever-growing greed, he turned her away, ignorant to the fact that she was the goddess herself.

The dryads became furious, and as anger whipped them into a frenzy they demanded a response from the goddess, who was livid with rage herself. Demeter vowed that from that day forward, Erysichthon's punishment was to suffer an insatiable hunger, and no meal, banquet or gift would allow him to feel full and content.

Thus, starting from daybreak the following morning, from the moment he woke to the moment he fell asleep with a rumbling stomach, the king would eat and eat, but would find no way to satiate his greed, which only grew and grew. As evening fell each day, starving and wild, the king would beg the skies for rest. But even in his sleep the king could not find respite, as every night he was sent nightmarish torments by Demeter in the form of the Oneiroi – black-winged spirits that plagued him in his dreams, tempting him with elaborate banquets and feasts.

Soon the king had but a crumb left in his food stores. He had eaten the crops barren, and roasted on a spit any animal that his servants could find him – sucking each bone so dry that they became splintered and marrowless. Such was his hunger he offered all of his money to those who would sell him food, which left him penniless. He even decided to sell his own beloved daughter, Mestra, for just one more bite to eat. Eventually – with nothing left to eat, nothing to sell and nothing left of his kingdom – Erysichthon devoured the only thing left – himself.

A myth is a *vehicle* for truth without necessarily *being* truthful, and can allow us to stare personal truths in the eye through deep and meaningful symbolism. This myth, although ancient, bears clear meaning to us in the modern world, and the resemblance between the greedy king and Western culture is easy for all to see. The simple and direct wisdom in these ancient words helps us to understand that our greed will only lead to one thing: the destruction of all that we hold dear, bit by bit, until we devour ourselves. The goddess is fair at first, and gives the king a chance. But, just like in other traditional cultural belief, the spirits will not hold back when they are disrespected. It is exactly this wisdom that reminds indigenous people the importance of staying in balance. A bleak reminder that we must be careful to balance our human tendency for greed with a healthy awe and fear of the natural world.

Simple but powerful stories such as the myth of King Erysichthon and the goddess Demeter are examples of how earth-centric practices can assist us in living in balance. I feel that one of the reasons that shamanism is becoming so popular is that many people are coming to their own conclusions: the way that we live in the West is unsustainable. Many also feel severed from their connection to the natural world. Practices like shamanism offer us a route out of our greed and back to connection with the earth and each other.

Going back to global warming, the cause of this from a shamanic sense is imbalance. The warming up of the earth is the response of the animate sun and earth to a huge lack of respect by large portions of humanity. For too long the spirits that represent the sun and earth have not been honoured, and we have destroyed too much natural habitat. While some do not believe in spirits, the scientific cause still offers the same symptom and outcome. Had humans not lived outside of their means and destroyed much of the earth's natural ecosystems – in order to burn natural resources to power their societies – the earth's weather systems would not have been altered to the potentially cataclysmic levels that they are now. Whichever way you look at it – through science or spirit – the response of the earth has been the same, and so is the answer: we must find a return to balance.

But this is a huge job, and no one person can do it alone. All we can do is make personal changes, and hope that the effects of them ripple outward positively. Animist and shamanic practice is a brilliant way to do this. A real benefit of beginning to honour natural powers, such as the sun, the earth, the wind or the rain, is that all of us already have our own relationships with them. They are not avant-garde concepts that we must find room for in our culture, but ever present in daily life. We need only to take some time to tune in, to remind ourselves that the world around us is conscious. What a beautiful gift it is that we can see the same sun, feel the same wind, rain and earth that have existed since the very beginning of time – to feel how our ancestors felt and experience the natural world as they did. What a gift it is also that we live in a time when we can be inspired by still-existing earth-centric cultures who have their wisdom intact, and can teach us how to come back to balance, to have more compassion for the natural world, and to find our peace again. Although the job is momentous in its scale, this should still bring comfort to us in the West. The answers are there for us, and this is a great place to be. We need only dedicate ourselves to the cause, and humbly utilise practices like shamanism and animism to begin to heal ourselves, our communities and our culture.

RITUAL 9

Singing Up the Sun

The final ritual in this book is a celebration of life.

Healing can seem so dark at times. As we confront our fears and soothe the parts of us that need the most love, difficult emotions arise to be seen, felt and heard, and we must develop the necessary inner compassion that can hold our pain in a way that transforms it.

Earth-centric spirituality reminds us that the beauty of the world can be transformative. Each day, the world renews itself from dark to light – this is deep symbolism for the opportunities that we have to transform ourselves. The cycles of night and day teach us that redemption, a second chance and new life, is always possible. Darkness will never last forever. If we persist, and give it time, our internal sun will rise again and we can bathe in the warmth of our own compassionate presence.

I find it beautiful that this vast world has revolved around the same sun forever. All of the cultures that inhabit this wonderful earth have looked to the same sun for guidance, hope and the warmth and light that it provides. The sun that we feel the warmth of each day is the same sun that our ancestors would have used to guide them across the landscape. It is the same sun that they danced under and honoured in ritual, and this still connects us all – as one family with one heart.

This is a beautiful and simple ritual that helps us to remember who we are and reconnect with our true essence and personal power, while honouring the most precious star in our universe.

WHAT YOU NEED

- A mat, blanket or sheepskin (if you have one)
- A pre-written song of honouring
- A percussive instrument – shaker/rattle/drum

INSTRUCTIONS

- Set your alarm so that you can get to a natural landmark where you are able to have an unobstructed view as the sun rises over the horizon. It helps to choose somewhere that has as uninterrupted a view as possible as the sun peeks over the earth. If you cannot do this, try to find a window in your home with the best view.

- Set down your mat, blanket or sheepskin and connect to a place of deep awareness within your body. You can lie on the earth or sit upright. Let any stresses, anxieties or worries temporarily fade away as you give yourself in service to the sun that provides so much to us on earth.

- As the sun starts to rise, play your percussive instrument and close your eyes, connecting yourself to the monotonous sounds, feeling them reverberate throughout your body.

- As the sun rises, sing your song from your heart directly to the sun – thanking it for your life, your family's life, your culture's existence and the land.
- Repeat this song three times and close your eyes, feeling the sun's warmth on your face and body.

Write down your experiences in your shamanic journal so that you can document how this makes you feel. This can include any bodily sensations, any thoughts or emotions that arise, or anything else that you deem important.

CONCLUSION

Rooting to the Earth – Growing Upwards

At this point in the book I hope that you have a much firmer understanding of earth-centric spiritualities, their usages in traditional contexts, and how we can start to see our own modern lives from these more ancient perspectives. By learning some of the basic tenets of earth-centric practice – giving offerings, connecting as a community, the importance of restoring our balance and putting the earth first – we can go a long way to begin remedying the issues that we all face.

Bringing this book full circle and back to personal healing – it is by putting these conditions in place and creating a cultural ecosystem that supports healing that we can let healing happen. In short, it is by becoming aware of the imbalances in our culture that we can begin to address them. Earth-centric spiritualities are not panaceas or perfect ways to live, but they do provide important guidance on how we can come back to an equilibrium as humans. Once we are there, it is up to us to decide what to do next.

Healing is actually quite passive, once the necessary conditions are in place and balance is restored. Healing does not need to be a struggle if the correct ecosystem is there. A plant will grow if the soil is full of nutrients, if the sunlight is adequate, if the water is available, and if there is space and room for it to flourish. When you grow a plant, you do not worry so much about whether the seed itself is capable of growing, but address the conditions to support it in doing so. We are much the same. For our personal healing, it is the conditions and foundations that must be remedied so we can settle back into balance and allow the psyche and the body to reconnect to the soul. We are not machines to be fixed, but complex organic organisms with spiritual needs that must come back to living in the way that we are meant to if we are to experience healing and growth. In many ways, we are now, as a Western culture, remembering and relearning what it really means to be human.

So I ask you this:

What is your sunlight?
Where is your water?
How is your soil?
Do you have space to grow?

* * *

Much of this book has been about looking backwards towards ancient traditions, or at cultures who still do things in 'the old ways'. I now encourage you, armed with this knowledge, to stay present with our culture as it is and look forward. For there comes a point when there is no use in looking backwards too far. Old traditions and ancestral wisdom are of vital importance, but only if they can be applied in the present day, in order to have beneficial effects on the future. Otherwise these things easily slip into becoming cosplay and escapism. We should also take care to not become lazy and seek to simply transplant still-existing traditions into our culture, expecting them to work in the same way. With huge reverence and honouring, we must listen to our indigenous cousins and take heed of their lessons, but not fall into the trap of mimicking what they do. This is a fine balance to tread, and one we will not always get right. We have to be patient, and understand that it will take many generations for our culture to develop spiritually. Our role at the beginning of this great Western spiritual journey is to lay strong enough foundations to allow this process to unfold organically. If our intention is strong enough, I am sure we will get there.

The Western ideals of attaining what we seek with immediate effect may not work when it comes to authentic spirituality, but there is huge solace in knowing that to heal ourselves and to rebalance our culture for future generations are the greatest gifts that we could ever bestow on those who will come after us. Some of the most breathtaking achievements of humanity were set in motion by people who understood that they would not be around to see the end result, and we now have the choice to be part of a sacred legacy in the West that may determine the state of our future world.

To do so we must remember the reasons why we utilise earth-centric practice. This is not weekend hobby spiritualism, but time-honoured and hugely powerful methods of working with the earth and its spiritual representations. These are forms of spiritual practice that were developed out of the need for survival. We must keep that in mind when we practise this way. Remembering this does not need to put a downer on things, or make them more serious than they need to be, but, conversely, it helps us to really celebrate and praise life when we perform our rituals and ceremonies, and to see the interconnectedness in all things in our daily lives. We must not practise with tension, but be calm and gracious in our honouring of the natural world and our ancestors. We will make mistakes, and be overzealous or over-ambitious, but these are all normal human behaviours that can provide great wisdom if we can become aware of them. In my experience, the spirits want us to be committed, and, if our hearts are in the right place and we are humble, they will be fair with us. The key is compassion, for it is when we become selfish, greedy and full of unchecked desire that we start to move away from our natural joyful states and get in trouble.

If we are able to start to understand our propensity for too much magical thinking and mind projection then we can begin to bring more practical wisdom and clarity into our lives. This helps to make things much more down-to-earth and accessible. In my own experience, this is where people who aren't drawn to spirituality start to become more interested. When they see that people who practise spirituality are just like them it gives them permission to get involved too. We need as many bridges from authentic spiritual practice to the modern world as we can, and if you can be the person from your tribe, family or community who is able to act as that bridge, then remember to be authentically you – this will emanate outward and inspire others to connect with their own unique power. As spoken about in previous chapters, it wasn't until I brought the two worlds together – the spiritual and the mundane – that my practices started to benefit me. Before that, as I wrongly believed that I had to become something to be spiritual, I descended into paranoia, confusion and loneliness, isolating myself from family and friends. This had hugely negative ramifications for me, and it doesn't need to be the case for you. Bring all of yourself to spirituality – believe me, there is room!

Much of the ability to bring all of ourselves to our

practice is bound up in how well we understand the stories that we are part of. Our personal, family, tribal and cultural stories. By seeing the sacredness in these stories and our unique and important role within them we start to empower ourselves. Knowing where you come from helps you to understand who you are, and knowing who you are helps you to feel confident in where you are going. These are not mere psychological exercises but symbolic anchors that greatly protect us from the trials and tribulations of life. Life is difficult for everyone – that much is certain – but if we can bring meaning and purpose to our struggles they can become more transformative. While this doesn't make our griefs any easier, we can make sure that they do not consume us, and we can rise out of the ashes of our personal pains like a phoenix. Suffering and loss are things we all share. The great burden of the gift of being alive is that nothing lasts forever, but we can find great comfort in the togetherness of celebrating life and its cycles of renewal amongst one another.

I implore you to develop a healthy cynicism with your spirituality. This will help to guard you from the endless promises of the business-minded parts of the New Age. All authentic traditional spiritualities can be verified. In short, they really work, and when they are not able to help they say so. Starting to see spirituality as something realistic is so important for us on our journey in the West. When the New Age promises extreme healing in short amounts of time, or when modern gurus who have everything figured out promise you miracle cures – take these things with a pinch of salt. If it seems too good to be true, it probably is. We must remember that, like all structures birthed out of capitalism, much of the New Age is set up for profit. Extreme prices and glamorous spirituality perhaps has its place somewhere, but for the vast majority of us practising this way is not authentic or attainable. Some may enjoy the enchantment and mystique of the New Age, but let us all remember that it does not always need to be this way. Spirituality and healing are our birthrights as humans, and down-to-earth, accessible and authentic spirituality should be available for everyone at all times. We are only as strong as the least advantaged members of our society – we must help whenever we can.

Finally, we understand that healing – however chaotic, confusing and gut-wrenchingly difficult – follows a three-fold path. The journey of severance, into the liminal, then aggregation – is part of life, and always has been. Within the personal maelstrom of our healing journey, we can always return to the dependable nature of this process – so I implore you to learn these concepts and understand what to expect and what must be done at each stage. However personal your healing may seem, it has played out a thousand times over time. You are not alone, and you don't need to figure everything out yourself.

It is my great wish that the words in these pages will have assisted you in some way, but I do not expect this book to be the final piece in the puzzle for anybody who reads it. You may now be inspired to take your knowledge of earth-centric practice further, and to move beyond the personal rituals provided in the book and perhaps even into your local animistic or shamanic communities.

This is a beautiful thing, and in my opinion where true and lasting healing can be found. A book can only hope to offer concepts, which can be extremely helpful, but at some point we must ground these concepts into our daily lives so that they become lived experiences rather than intellectual ideas.

I encourage you to seek out like-minded individuals and find your own earth-centric communities. They are growing in the West and are never too far away, no matter where we live. The internet is an incredible resource too, and many traditional cultures now come to the West to share wisdom and their spiritual concepts, and to perform healing ceremonies. Earth-centric spirituality is a vast topic, and there are many avenues to explore and draw inspiration from.

As a last note, I want to remind you of this quote about healing from the very beginning of our adventure through these pages together.

> Although this book is about healing, life is not. Life is about existing naturally in the organic and balanced way that nature functions. Healing, then, in

the way that is meant in this book, is about dusting off the old pathways that lead us back to that balance. It is important we remember that healing is not the *goal* in life, but the necessary step that we must sometimes take when we find ourselves stranded away from where we feel we are meant to be.

Safe travels, and my door is always open.

SOURCES

'1 in 5 British adults say they've had an affair', YouGov (27 May 2015): https://yougov.co.uk/society/articles/12404-one-five-british-adults-admit-affair?redirect_from=%2Ftopics%2Fsociety%2Farticles-reports%2F2015%2F05%2F27%2Fone-five-british-adults-admit-affair

Baker, Carl, and Kirk-Wade, Esme, 'Mental health statistics: prevalence, services and funding in England', House of Commons Library (13 March 2023): https://researchbriefings.files.parliament.uk/documents/SN06988/SN06988.pdf

Booth, Robert, Aguilar García, Carmen, and Duncan, Pamela, 'Shamanism, pagans and wiccans: trends from the England and Wales census', *Guardian* (29 November 2022): https://www.theguardian.com/uk-news/2022/nov/29/ten-things-weve-learned-from-the-england-and-wales-census

Holt-Lunstad, Julianne, Smith, Timothy B., and Layton, J. Bradley, 'Social relationships and mortality risk: a meta-analytic review', *PLOS Medicine* 7(7) (2010): https://www.ncbi.nlm.nih.gov/pmc/articles/PMC2910600/

'Jiddu Krishnamurti biography', Age of the Sage: https://www.age-of-the-sage.org/theosophy/krishnamurti.html

Jung, Carl, 'The Philosophical Tree', in *The Collected Works of C.G. Jung*, vol. 13 (Routledge & Kegan Paul, 1967)

Lynch, Terry, 'The sophistication of a primitive people', *Irish Times* (9 December 2008): https://www.irishtimes.com/news/health/the-sophistication-of-a-primitive-people-1.921473

Melton, J. Gordon, 'New Age movement: Realizing the New Age', Britannica.com: https://www.britannica.com/topic/New-Age-movement/Realizing-the-New-Age

'Mental health of children and young people in England 2022- wave 3 follow up to the 2017 survey', NHS Digital (29 November 2022): https://digital.nhs.uk/data-and-information/publications/statistical/mental-health-of-children-and-young-people-in-england/2022-follow-up-to-the-2017-survey

Naftulin, Julia, 'Gwyneth Paltrow sent her employees to take psychedelic mushrooms in Jamaica. One staffer said she felt like she'd undergone 5 years of therapy', Insider (24 January 2020): https://www.insider.com/goop-staffers-went-on-a-psychedelic-mushroom-retreat-in-jamaica-2020-1

'Non-religious surge: 37% tick "No religion" in 2021 Census – UK among least religious countries in the world', Humanists UK (29 November 2022): https://humanists.uk/2022/11/29/non-religious-surge-37-tick-no-religion-in-2021-census-uk-among-least-religious-countries-in-the-world/

San Sebastián, Miguel, and Hurtig, Anna-Karin, 'Cancer among indigenous people in the Amazon Basin of Ecuador, 1985–2000', *Pan American Journal of Public Health* 16(5) (2004): https://pubmed.ncbi.nlm.nih.gov/15729982/

'Sense of belonging helps people suffering depression', *Michigan News* (6 April 2005): https://news.umich.edu/sense-of-belonging-helps-people-suffering-depression/

Sinha, Rajita, 'New findings on biological factors predicting addiction relapse vulnerability', *Current Psychiatry Reports* 13(5) (2011): https://www.ncbi.nlm.nih.gov/pmc/articles/PMC3674771/

'Sting reveals " playful" sex secrets', *Evening Standard* (11 April 2012): https://www.standard.co.uk/showbiz/sting-reveals-playful-sex-secrets-6555654.html

Trafton, Anne, 'A hunger for social contact', *MIT News* (23 November 2020): https://news.mit.edu/2020/hunger-social-cravings-neuroscience-1123

'Young people more and more "spiritual," not more religious', In Trust: https://intrust.org/Resources/Blog/entryid/125/young-people-more-and-more-spiritual-not-more-religious

Yurday, Erin, 'Divorce statistics UK 2023', NimbleFins (20 June 2023): https://www.nimblefins.co.uk/divorce-statistics-uk

ACKNOWLEDGEMENTS

This book would not have been possible unless it was for the hard work and support of many people.

Thank you to my wonderful family for always encouraging me, and my beautiful wife, Ruth, who has supported me resolutely and patiently listened to each edit of this book with open and eager ears.

Thank you to all of my teachers over the years who have assisted me in my explorations through spirituality and in my own healing journey.

Thank you to Charlie Brotherstone, Holly Whitaker, Jessica Anderson and Celia Hayley – all who helped me in huge ways to get my original rabble of ideas together into something coherent.

It has been a dream come true to write this book, and I hope that there will be more to come.

ABOUT THE AUTHOR

©Ruth Garner

EDDY ELSEY is a British shamanic healer and author, and is the found of Street Spirituality. He has been featured in *GQ, Men's Health, Tatler, Women's Health,* the *Evening Standard* and more, as well as being named as *Tatler*'s 'Best healer for transformation'.

He has trained extensively in shamanic practice with renowned teachers in the West and in the East, and offers donation-based healings from his home in London, as well as running talks and workshops around the world.

Eddy represents a bridge between ancient knowledge and the modern world and is passionate about interlacing authentic spiritual wellness and everyday life. His down-to-earth nature and relatability bring an empowering stance to those on their healing journey, while providing them with an accessible way to harness the power of authentic spiritual practice.

You can find him at streetspirituality.com.